# JUDGING THE JUDGES

Judge John T. Noonan speaks at the University of Notre Dame in 2009. PHOTO COURTESY OF THE ARCHIVES OF THE U.S. COURT OF APPEALS FOR THE NINTH CIRCUIT

# JUDGING THE JUDGES

John T. Noonan, Jr.

CAROLINA ACADEMIC PRESS
Durham, North Carolina

LIBRARY OF CONGRESS CATALOGING-IN-PUBLICATION DATA
Names: Noonan, John T., Jr. (John Thomas), 1926–2017 author
Title: Judging the judges / John T. Noonan, Jr.
Description: Durham, North Carolina : Carolina Academic Press. LLC, 2025. | Includes bibliographical references and index.
Identifiers: LCCN 2025035202 | ISBN 9781531031367 paperback | ISBN 9781531031374 ebook
Subjects: LCSH: Noonan, John T., Jr. (John Thomas), 1926–2017—Political and social views | Judicial process—United States | Judicial ethics—United States | Justice, Administration of—United States | Judges—United States
Classification: LCC KF8775 .N66 2025 | DDC 347.73/14—dc23/eng/20250805
LC record available at https://lccn.loc.gov/2025035202

Carolina Academic Press
700 Kent Street
Durham, North Carolina 27701
(919) 489-7486
www.cap-press.com

Printed in the United States of America

# Contents

# Preface

*Persons and Masks of the Law*, a classic statement of John Noonan's jurisprudence, was published fifty years ago, developing themes he had explored in his 1972 Oliver Wendell Holmes, Jr. Lectures at Harvard Law School. Now, embracing his life in the law as both a professor and judge, *Judging the Judges* is the fruit of his thirty years on the United States Court of Appeals for the Ninth Circuit, his personal effort to serve these principles. Together these two books stand as bookends of theory and practice in his evolving jurisprudence.

Between roughly 2006 and 2016, Judge Noonan selected a small group of cases from his judicial experience, stories that he thought illustrated life on the bench, as well as illuminating his philosophy of law, and cases that have "a complexity, density, and ambiguity that the simplification of hypotheticals lack." He also saw these stories as a defense of the Ninth Circuit, which was constantly the object of political criticism and repeated efforts to split the circuit.

A story can be a remarkable tool: entertaining, teaching, and, as it sparks facts and characters back to life, even contributing to a search for justice. Whether he was at the dinner table, walking in the Berkeley hills, or discussing issues with his colleagues, Judge Noonan was a master storyteller. Sadly, he died in April of 2017 before *Judging the Judges*, his collection of stories from the bench, was ready for publication.

I am profoundly grateful to two special people who, in different ways, have rescued Judge Noonan's manuscript from oblivion. First, his loyal secretary at the court, Evelyn Lew, saved and organized everything that was related to this lengthy and frequently interrupted project. Every list, every draft, and each revision was forwarded to me when his chambers closed. When I finally managed to confront the challenge, I turned to Jeff Powell at the Duke University School of Law for help. I knew particularly of his admiration for *Persons and Masks of the Law* and its use in his courses. Judge Noonan's kindred spirit, he responded with incredible generosity and grace. The book you hold in your hands would not exist were it not for his editing and the focus of his Introduction.

**MARY LEE NOONAN**
BERKELEY, CALIFORNIA

# Introduction

## The Author

Judge John T. Noonan, Jr., was a distinguished figure in the history of the American judiciary. A few months before President Ronald Reagan nominated Noonan in 1985 to serve on the United States Court of Appeals for the Ninth Circuit, an article in *Newsweek* described him as "[u]niquely gifted as a moralist, historian and lawyer ... [someone who] challenges American jurisprudence with a rare humanistic vision."[1] After Noonan had been a judge for over a decade, the brilliant and polymathic Judge Richard A. Posner wrote that Noonan was probably one of the two "most distinguished living judges, who before ascending the bench, made important contributions as academics to both jurisprudence and moral theory."[2] Several years after Noonan's death in 2017, another writer commented that "[o]ver the course of three decades on the Ninth Circuit ... Judge Noonan established himself as one of America's most original, insightful, and genuinely empathetic judges."[3]

1. Kenneth L. Woodward, Noonan's Life of the Law, *Newsweek*, Apr. 1, 1985, at 82.

2. Richard A. Posner, *Reply to Critics of the Problematics of Moral and Legal Theory*, 111 Harv. L. Rev. 1796, 1796 (1998). The other distinguished scholar-judge Posner named was Harvard law professor and Massachusetts Supreme Judicial Court Justice Charles Fried.

3. Charles J. Reid, Jr., *Judge John T. Noonan, Jr. v. Joe Arpaio*, 17 U. St. Thomas L.J. 993, 993 (2022). The significance of Professor Reid's reference to Judge Noonan's empathetic capacity will become clear.

Many other quotations could be marshalled to make the point that John Noonan was a major figure not only as a judge and legal scholar but also as an intellectual historian and moral philosopher. In 2001, the great civil liberties lawyer and scholar Norman Dorsen correctly observed that "[s]everal of his books are classics: *The Scholastic Analysis of Usury*, *Contraception*, *Persons and Masks of the Law*, and *Bribes*."[4] I would add to that list, at the very least, Judge Noonan's "magnificent book on the legal controversy surrounding slaves on *The Antelope*,"[5] as well as his history of American religious freedom, *The Lustre of Our Country*, and his exploration of change and continuity in Catholic moral thought, *A Church that Can and Cannot Change*.[6]

Broad-ranging as John Noonan's scholarship was, twin themes run throughout it: the centrality of persons to any adequate account of moral or legal action, and the consequent rejection of all attempts to escape the reality of human relationships into a world of abstractions or ideas. "[I]t is necessary to insist that the person precedes analysis," he wrote in the original foreword to *Persons and Masks of the Law*, "responsibility comes in the response to other persons."[7] Noonan was painfully aware how tempting it is in the law to focus on bloodless rules and principles and so hide the reality that law involves some persons making decisions that may inflict suffering or even death on other persons. "Those who suppose that the legal universe is a self-subsistent set of rules existing outside of its participants and constraining lawyers and judges to act against their consciences will always be prevalent among lawyers, judges

---

4. Norman Dorsen, *John T. Noonan, Jr.: Renaissance Man in the Catholic Tradition*, 76 Notre Dame L. Rev. 843, 844 (2001). The books Dorsen characterized as classics are *The Scholastic Analysis of Usury* (1957), *Contraception: A History of Its Treatment by the Catholic Theologians and Canonists* (1965, expanded ed. 1986), *Persons and Masks of the Law: Cardozo, Holmes, Jefferson and Wythe as Makers of the Masks* (1976, 2d ed. 2002), and *Bribes* (1984).

5. Sanford Levinson, *Speaking in the Name of the Law: Some Reflections on Professional Responsibility and Judicial Accountability*, 1 St. Thomas L.J. 447, 448 (2003). The Supreme Court decision that was the subject of Noonan's book was *The Antelope*, 23 U.S. (10 Wheat.) 66 (1825).

6. *The Antelope: The Ordeal of the Recaptured Africans in the Administrations of James Monroe and John Quincy Adams* (1977), *The Lustre of Our Country: The American Experience of Religious Freedom* (1998), and *A Church that Can and Cannot Change: The Development of Catholic Moral Teaching* (2005).

7. *Persons and Masks* (2d ed.) xix–xx.

and legal historians."[8] Resisting that temptation in his work as a scholar, Professor Noonan pioneered a method of writing legal history that directs attention to the individuals involved in cases and controversies and the contingencies that influence or even determine the application of ostensibly general rules.

*Persons and Masks of the Law* is John Noonan's best known application of this method written before he became a judge. In that book, as he wrote many years later:

> I distinguished between persons, roles, and masks. Persons were flesh and blood and soul, touchable human beings. Roles were the particular parts the persons played in society, parts defined by law or custom. Mask was a metaphor I chose to express suppression by law of the human identity of the person playing the role. At one end of the social scale, the mask of property had for centuries suppressed the human identity of a slave. As property, he or she could be owned, bought, sold, and used as a tool without the user acknowledging the human person affected. The legal mask, almost perfectly, obscured that person.
>
> At the other end of society, the mask of sovereignty hid those exercising the powers of government. A sovereign was not accountable for certain of his acts. As the embodiment, the sovereign was immune. Again, focus on the mask created by law almost perfectly concealed the human actor behind it.
>
> There were also, I had suggested, less complete masks provided by legal systems—Plaintiffs and defendants, for example. Analyzing cases in terms of Ps and Ds permitted a law teacher to ignore the individuality of litigants while expounding a rule. Similarly, a judge's thought could move from the persons to classes of Ps and Ds. The line between a mask and a role was imprecise. Roles could be turned, more or less effectively, into masks. But roles were as essential as rules to the functioning of a society. Masks were a problem and a plague. I argued that a fuller and better understanding of a case was achieved by taking into account the actual participants, the persons who were submerged in categories.[9]

8. *The Antelope* 159.

9. Judge Noonan apparently wrote this summary of *Persons and Masks* with a view to using it in the foreword to *Judging the Judges*, but it is not in the last version of the

*Persons and Masks* demonstrated in rich detail the ways in which "masks," in Noonan's sense, obscured the personal and moral dimensions in the Virginia law of slavery that Thomas Jefferson and George Wythe shaped, and in two famous cases, *American Banana Co. v. United Fruit Co.* and *Palsgraf v. Long Island R. Co.*, with Justice Oliver Wendell Holmes and Chief Judge Benjamin N. Cardozo writing for their respective courts.[10] A fourth case study was originally intended as another chapter in *Persons and Masks* but expanded to book length and was published a year after as the separate volume *The Antelope*.[11] In it, Noonan painstakingly traced out the years-long ordeal of 280 Africans who were found in chains onboard a ship involved in the slave trade, an ordeal that led to an opinion by Chief Justice John Marshall writing for an ostensibly unanimous Supreme Court, but (as Noonan showed) did not end there if one is concerned with persons and not just with legal rulings abstracted from their facts.[12]

As by-then Judge Noonan explained in a new preface to the re-issue of *Persons and Masks* a quarter-century after its original publication, that book drew on his experience as a lawyer and legal scholar and "was an argument as to how the legal process should be understood... taught [and] remembered... not about how to decide a case." How we should

---

foreword. For the full text of the separate document in which the summary is found, see Appendix D.

10. Jefferson needs no introduction other than to note that he and Wythe were members of the committee appointed by the Virginia legislature (pursuant to a motion introduced by Jefferson) to revise the commonwealth's laws, including the laws related to slavery. Wythe was a legendarily learned lawyer who personally trained many founding-era members of the state bar including Jefferson, the first American law professor, and chancellor on the Virginia High Court of Chancery from 1777 until his death in 1806. Holmes wrote for eight justices (the ninth concurred only in the result) in *American Banana Co.*, 213 U.S. 347 (1909), holding that the Sherman Antitrust Act did not apply to sovereign acts of a foreign country outside the United States. *Palsgraf*, 248 N.Y. 339 (1928), was a landmark tort decision on "proximate cause," holding that the defendant railroad was not liable to the severely injured plaintiff for the unforeseeable consequences of its employees' actions; Cardozo wrote for a bare majority of the New York Court of Appeals.

11. The case was *The Antelope*, 23 U.S. (10 Wheat.) 66 (1825).

12. The book carefully traces the events before and after the ship's capture—the experiences of the captives, the stakeholders and lawyers involved in the eventual litigation over their fate, and political developments in Congress and the president's cabinet bearing on the case. Very little of this would appear in most treatments of the case. For Noonan's demonstration that the Supreme Court's unanimity was a façade, see *The Antelope* 105–16.

understand and remember and teach law and legal history are quintessential academic questions, and in writing his books, Professor Noonan had taken the appropriate academic perspective on his subject. *Persons and Masks of the Law* and its spin-off volume *The Antelope* were not written from the perspective of an academic imagining him or herself as a judge, and thus they did not try to address directly a judge's questions. Nor could they have done so with complete success: as Judge Noonan later wrote, at the end of the description of *Persons and Masks* quoted above: "Being a law professor and not a judge at the time I did not note the mask of the judge. Taught by experience, I am now conscious of the judge's . . . "—the sentence breaks off, and we do not know with certainty how Noonan meant to complete it.[13] In context, however, we can assume that he had in mind, at least in part, the observations he had just made, that roles—including the judicial role—are "as essential as rules to the functioning of a society," but that roles can also "be turned, more or less effectively, into masks," which are "a problem and a plague." Perhaps something like "I am now conscious of the judge's need to act within his role without donning a mask" captures at least part of Noonan's thought.

Fifteen years' experience as a judge, the new preface to *Persons and Masks* continued, had led John Noonan to regret somewhat the professorial criticism of Jefferson, Wythe, Holmes, and Cardozo "implied by an emphasis on facts that were not their focus."

> The central question for me is not implied criticism of the lawmakers and opinion writers. It is the place of rules in the legal system if the process takes persons into account. [*Persons and Masks*] defends rules as indispensable. But if rules are indispensable, does not taking persons into account distort the process by bending the rules to fit the persons? This question I will answer from experience.[14]

The four pages that followed in the new preface are extremely interesting but too brief to treat as a full answer to Judge Noonan's central question. The logic of Noonan's creative method of writing legal history, that a deep examination of the persons and circumstances and context of specific cases is necessary truly to understand the legal process,

13. Appendix D, page 144.
14. *Persons and Masks* (2d ed.) ix–x.

applies just as much to answering the question whether judges can take persons into account without stepping out of their properly rule-bound role. To say what it is like to be a judge, and to address his central question about how judges *should* take persons into account, would require John Noonan (by his own lights) to write another book, one similar to *Persons and Masks* and *The Antelope*, but from the judge's perspective, informed by the judge's experience.

## The Manuscript

Within a decade of his appointment to the Ninth Circuit, Judge Noonan apparently had such a book in mind. In 1995, a friend wrote in a "brief biography" of the judge published as a journal article that "[u]sing his life as a stimulus to research and reflection, he is also meditating a book on judicial practice."[15] At some, perhaps much later, point, Noonan himself sketched the outline of a book tentatively titled *What It Is Like to Be a Judge*.[16] The project in view was tremendously ambitious. The outline begins with seven chapter titles, six of which are identifiable as chapters that he wrote and are in this volume. Their placement in the outline was highly significant: although Noonan planned to go on to address issues arranged by conceptual content rather than individual case, *What It Is Like to Be a Judge* was to begin where John Noonan the professor and John Noonan the judge believed law ought to begin and end, with persons and their responsibilities as persons to one another.

Following the seven case-study chapter titles are twenty-seven topic headings, many with brief annotations ("Themes") giving further indication of their anticipated content. We can guess with some confidence what some of these sections would have addressed. Number 17, "Does The Judge Make A Difference," points to a recurrent theme in *Judging the Judges*, the importance of the individual who sits as the trial judge or as

15. Kevin Starr, *Judge John T. Noonan, Jr. A Brief Biography*, 11 J.L. & Religion 151, 176 (1995).

16. The outline is reproduced in Appendix A. It is not dated, although the reference to neuroscience suggests that Judge Noonan may have written it at roughly the same time (2000–01) he foresaw the future value of "the neurosciences" to understanding "what is central to law, the human mind." See the following note.

a member of the appellate panel, or who votes whether to take a case en banc or decide what weight to give a decision in a later case. (Noonan's answer was a resounding "Yes!"). Other headings are a mystery: what indeed is "The Secret Of The System" (number 23)?

Some of the topic headings show just how broad a study Noonan intended. Number 1, "Intent," has as one of its themes "Neuroscience," and as it happens, Judge Noonan wrote two articles commending an understanding of the neurosciences as critical in the near future to legal education and to the work of judges.[17] The first theme noted for Number 11, "Judges as Models," is "Cardozo; Hand, Jackson." Noonan's admiration for Cardozo, Learned Hand, and Robert Jackson, was evident, but it would have been fascinating to have him explain more fully his reasons, particularly since he was politely critical of Cardozo and Hand on the role of metaphor in legal thought and writing.[18]

---

17. *See* John T. Noonan, Jr., *Judicial Reflections on Today's Legal Education*, 15 St. John's J. Legal Comment. 329, 330 (2001) ("I think today [law students] should have some serious exposure to one of the sciences, in particular I would say the neurosciences. The neurosciences will be to this century what physics were to the last century. The neurosciences are dealing with how the brain works. They are taking on what we used to take for granted, the mental apparatus with which we analyze the law and legal states of mind. We have to know what the neurosciences have to say."); John T. Noonan, Jr., *Judges As Scholars: Are They? Should They Be?*, 84 Judicature 7, 47 (2000) ("the neurosciences are already at work investigating what is central to law, the human mind; and their successes, while limited, hold great promise for the next century. What physics was to the twentieth, the neurosciences will be to the twenty-first. Such at least is the expectation.... Dependent as judges are on the recollection of observers, on the intentions inferred from actions, on the constructions put on human acts, we should not be unaware of the basic processes by which memory is made, intentions formed, acts performed. Recently, the California Center for Judicial Education and Research sponsored a three-day seminar on genetics for both state and federal judges at Berkeley; DNA as a forensic tool was an important practical topic. But more basic for our system of law than DNA will be work affecting our understanding of how the mind itself does its business.").

18. John T. Noonan, Jr., *Education, Intelligence, and Character in Judges*, 71 Minn. L. Rev. 1119, 1130 (1987) ("Cardozo's whole judicial career may be read as a struggle... to show, in his own actions as a judge, justice in the most unalloyed, incorruptible form. Patience in adversity—fortitude—was Cardozo's conspicuous virtue as he successfully undertook this mission."); John T. Noonan, Jr., *Choice of A Profession*, 21 Pepp. L. Rev. 381, 382 (1994) ("Judge Learned Hand, one of the great figures of an earlier time"); John T. Noonan, Jr., *The Relation of Words to Power*, 70 St. John's L. Rev. 13, 18 (1996) ("my favorite Supreme Court Justice, Robert Jackson... combined the ability to write with the ability to express a humanity resident in the community if a judge looks for it, not automatically accepting the overt community values, but inducing those underlying values that make us a people."). For Judge Noonan's criticism of Cardozo and Hand on metaphor, *see*

For whatever reasons, Judge Noonan never wrote *What It Is Like to Be a Judge*. But a few years before he died, he completed and then set aside, an almost complete manuscript that was, at least in part, the fulfilment and indeed an expansion of the first, case-study section he had projected for *What It Is Like to Be a Judge*. The present volume presents this manuscript under the title *Judging the Judges.*

On September 8, 2013, Judge Noonan dated a foreword to a manuscript that he clearly had been working on for some time—as noted above, six of the manuscript's chapters were included in the outline of *What It Is Like to Be a Judge*. The manuscript included a title page, reading "Ninth Circuit!" with a 2013 copyright notice in Noonan's name, and a table of contents listing fifteen chapters.[19] The manuscript was clearly not finished. Noonan had made several attempts to draft a foreword: there is another version dated April 2, 2013, that may be complete, and several apparent fragments exist; as explained below, the September foreword described the overall book in terms of an immediate controversy and did not fully represent the breadth of Noonan's accomplishment.[20] Chapter 11 in the table of contents and in the manuscript text ("The Judge is a Lazy Fellow") was, uniquely, not a case narrative, and much of its substance had been incorporated into the September 8 foreword; presumably Noonan had changed his mind about interrupting the sequence of case studies.[21] The table of contents listed a final, fifteenth chapter, "The Imaginary Stash House," that was not in the manuscript. When Noonan dated the September foreword,

---

Noonan, *Judges as Scholars*, 84 Judicature at 47 ("Two famous judges—Cardozo and Learned Hand—are on record as deploring the deceits of metaphor in the law. But is there any escape from metaphor? George Lakoff, professor of linguistics at Berkeley, has shown how basic to mental life are the metaphors derived from our body and our body's sense of space. Gerald Edelman, the neuroscientist, has surmised that the mind's natural movement is to metaphor."); Noonan, *The Relation of Words to Power*, 70 St. John's L. Rev. at 13 ("I have always been puzzled by a famous line of Learned Hand's putting down metaphor as invariably deceptive. Metaphor is unavoidable. The law is honeycombed with metaphor and we could not live without it.").

19. The table of contents gave the chapters in the same order as the chapters in this volume, with a chapter 11 that has been moved to Appendix E and a chapter 15 that is not extant. See below at notes 21 and 22.

20. The April foreword is in Appendix B, the September foreword in Appendix C, and the fragments are collected in Appendix D.

21. The text of this chapter has been moved to Appendix E.

a case called *United States v. Black* involving the government's use of a fictitious stash house as part of a sting operation had been argued and was under submission to a Ninth Circuit panel of which he was a member. A month and a half later, the decision was announced over a strong Noonan dissent, and it seems clear that he intended to turn the case into this final chapter, but no text is extant.[22]

Aside from these structural issues, the September 2013 manuscript presented few editorial challenges. Obvious typographical and similar errors have been corrected without notice, and the few other changes are flagged in a footnote. All footnotes to the manuscript and appendices are editorial, and are intended to supply information the reader may find useful.[23]

## The Lasting Significance of This Book

The September 2013 foreword to the manuscript, included here as an appendix, clearly identifies the book as an *apologia*, a defense of John Noonan's court against the accusation that the Ninth Circuit was a wayward, hyper-liberal court in almost outright rebellion against the Supreme Court. Read as an *apologia* for the Ninth Circuit at the time the foreword was dated, the manuscript is highly persuasive. Judge Noonan's candid and sometimes (self-)critical discussion of his own thinking and the actions and interactions of his colleagues are a convincing portrayal of a court that, whatever the flaws and foibles of its members, was col-

22. *Black*, 733 F.3d 294 (9th Cir. 2013), was argued on January 16, 2013, and the opinions were filed on October 23. Two years later the Ninth Circuit decided a similar case, *United States v. Pedrin*, 797 F.3d 792 (9th Cir. 2015), *on denial of rehearing en banc*, 806 F.3d 1009 (9th Cir. 2015), over Judge Noonan's vigorous dissent. His opinions in *Black* and *Pedrin* give a partial sense of what "The Imaginary Stash House" chapter might have said, and excerpts from them are included as the last chapter.

23. "[F]ootnoting can degenerate into pedantry." John T. Noonan, Jr., *Law Reviews*, 47 Stan. L. Rev. 1117, 1118 (1995). A friend of Judge Noonan once wrote that "John's books provide erudite fun in the reading. They must have been fun to write. It should be apparent that they are neither conventional history nor conventional legal writing." Robert E. Rodes, Jr., *An Overview of the Scholarship in Law and Religion of Judge John T. Noonan, Jr.*, 12 J.L. & Religion 533, 538 (1996). *Judging the Judges* confirms Professor Rodes's observation about the pleasure of reading a Noonan book.

lectively engaged in an intelligent, good faith attempt to administer the law in accordance with the limited role of its judges in the American legal system.[24] But the Ninth Circuit of the manuscript's case studies is quickly receding into the past, not least because John Noonan is no longer a member. Beyond providing "erudite fun in the reading,"[25] what is the lasting significance of this book?

The answer lies in the manuscript's obvious connection to the comprehensive account of *What It Is Like to Be a Judge* that Judge Noonan had at an earlier point intended to write. In 2000, after he had been a judge for almost fifteen years, Noonan wrote an article discussing the role of scholarship in the life of a judge. He first gave what he termed a "broad" definition of judicial scholarship: "reflective writing, not primarily designed to resolve a case or to entertain, but intended to instruct publicly... undertaken by judges." But he immediately "turn[ed] from these abstractions to three classic examples" of such scholarship, Justice Joseph Story's 1833 treatise on constitutional law, Justice Oliver Wendell Holmes's 1897 article *The Path of the Law*, and

> Benjamin Cardozo, *The Nature of the Judicial Process*, originally given by an associate judge of the Court of Appeals of New York as the Storrs Lectures at Yale Law School, and published as a book in 1923, the single best account of the job of a judge by a judge.[26]

As we've already seen, Noonan was a great admirer of Cardozo, and his description of Cardozo's book as "the single best account of the job of a judge by a judge," coming after having extensive judicial experience of his own, was high praise indeed. But as we also saw, Noonan was not an uncritical admirer of Cardozo, and we can identify with some confidence an aspect of Cardozo's account of the role of the judge with which Noonan sharply disagreed.

---

24. The statistics do not support the claim that the Supreme Court was dramatically more likely to reverse the Ninth Circuit than some other federal courts of appeals in the years prior to 2013. *See* https://ballotpedia.org/SCOTUS_case_reversal_rates_(2007_-_Present) (2024). *See also* Ilva Shapiro & Nathan Harvey, Break Up the Ninth Circuit, 26 Geo. Mason L. Rev. 1299, 1317–19 (2019) (labeling as a "myth" the charge that the Ninth Circuit was pursuing a partisan agenda).

25. Rodes, *An Overview of the Scholarship*, 12 J.L. & Religion at 538.

26. Noonan, *Judges as Scholars*, 84 Judicature at 7. 1923 is a typographical error for 1921.

*The Nature of the Judicial Process* is overwhelmingly general and abstract in its discussion of judicial decision making. Cardozo often refers to cases, but usually because there is some language he wishes to quote, and his discussion is brief and abstracting when he mentions any details. Late in the book, Cardozo admits that he has "thrown, perhaps too much, into the background the cases where the controversy turns not upon the rule of law, but upon its application to the facts."

> Those cases, after all, make up the bulk of the business of the courts. They are important for the litigants concerned in them. They call for intelligence and patience and reasonable discernment on the part of the judges who must decide them. But they leave jurisprudence where it stood before. As applied to such cases, the judicial process, as was said at the outset of these lectures, is a process of search and comparison, and little else.[27]

And Cardozo, however conscientious in deciding such cases with intelligence and patience and reasonable discernment, simply isn't very interested in them. Deciding them is a duty, and perhaps a somewhat wearying one. As he had indeed said very early in his lectures, Cardozo's real interests lay elsewhere, in what the judge can make out of the petty disputes that come before him: "the sordid controversies of litigants are the stuff out of which great and shining truths will ultimately be shaped. The accidental and the transitory will yield the essential and the permanent."[28]

It is impossible to imagine John Noonan writing or thinking about the cases before him, before any judge, as "the sordid controversies of litigants" to be made into something beautiful by leaving behind the "accidental and transitory"—in other words, what matters to the actual persons caught up in the legal process—to achieve "great and shining truths." *Judging the Judges* is a sustained refutation, or correction if you prefer, of Cardozo's abstraction away from persons to principles. It is precisely in the judge's recognition of the other persons involved in the judicial process, and above all of those who must personally bear the consequences of the court's decision, that the judge fulfills his or her

27. Cardozo, *The Nature of the Judicial Process* 104–05 (1921).
28. *Id.* at 18.

role. *Judging the Judges* is John Noonan's "account of the job of a judge by a judge," an account that corrects Cardozo's because Noonan does not lose sight of the judge's responsibility toward other persons.

> A judge's job is to affix responsibility—responsibility for a crime, a tort, a default, an error. The judge regularly places responsibility on the persons before the court. In this book, I seek to affix responsibility on the judge. Is the judge then to be judged? Why not? Self-judgment is not barred by judicial immunity....
>
> The judge is a person interacting with other persons—his colleagues, the lawyers in the case, and the litigants, whom an appeals court may not even see. The interaction involves rules that define the roles of the participants in the process and rules determining the law governing the case. A judge is given authority by his role. A judge is given direction by the law. Neither role nor law exhausts nor extinguishes the judge as person.[29]

Long before he wrote this book, Noonan expressed the hope that "every so often in a human heart the ice will crack, and a human person will acknowledge his responsibility for other human beings he has touched."[30] *Judging the Judges* sets out his argument that this hope can be realized in the judicial process, and if it can, of course it should be. That is a message for all times, all courts, and all of us.

## Acknowledgments

Two 2025 Duke Law School graduates, Damiloda Alada (LL.M.) and Jack Massih, provided great research assistance in compiling, respectively, annotated reviews of *Persons and Masks* and of *The Nature of the Judicial Process*, and a bibliography of Judge Noonan's voluminous writings. My librarian colleague Wick Shreve displayed his usual wizardry at finding documents that were beyond my reach, and my wonderful assistant Taylor Clark solved multiple, time-consuming formatting issues with the documents. At Carolina Academic Press, Keith and Scott Sipe gave me indispensable guidance and unfailing support, and

29. See below, pages 139–40.
30. *The Antelope* 159.

Ryland Bowman and Steve Oliva displayed their remarkable artistry by turning an electronic file into a beautiful book. My dear friend David Lange gave me invaluable advice in thinking about this project. As always, that amazing lawyer Sarah Powell, to whom I have the good fortune to be married, was a constant sounding board. I am grateful to each of them. And most of all, I want to thank Mary Lee Noonan for entrusting me with the tremendous privilege of preparing her husband's manuscript for publication.

**H. JEFFERSON POWELL**
DURHAM, NORTH CAROLINA

# JUDGING THE JUDGES

ONE

# The Electrician Who'd Read the Constitution[1]

HE HAD READ IT, ACTUALLY, IN THE PUBLIC LIBRARY of Quincy, Massachusetts, as he testified in his own defense while being tried for the federal felony of failing to file an income tax return. He had found that the Fourth Amendment forbade searches by the government without a warrant and that the Fifth Amendment states that you cannot be compelled to be a witness against yourself. He had relied on each of these propositions in concluding that the Constitution prevented the federal government from making him file a tax return. Requiring the return was searching him without a warrant. It was also making him, at least potentially, incriminate himself.

Few people do read the Constitution. Very few read it without prompting. Almost nobody comes up with a counter-cultural interpretation without coaching. The best guess by those familiar with this sort of case was that he had been exposed to tax protester literature popular in some branch of the electricians' trade. Tax protester literature runs in this way by occupation, just as particular heresies would run through a trade like the wool carders in medieval Italy. An argument that catches one member of the guild will catch another. The group has solidarity in resenting officious intrusion into its world. The tax protester believes as firmly as the medieval heretic that he has been enlightened. He and like-minded fellows are breaking out of a giant conspiracy that surrounds

1. The proceedings in the electrician's case are unpublished.

them. To be saved he has to be faithful to the light that he has received on being directed to a true understanding of the governing text.

The case was the first I had ever tried as a judge. I'd been on the bench two years and had voted on some 300 appeals. But I had never sat in court and presided over the battle in which facts are testified to and the person is present, flesh and blood, whom the prosecutor is seeking to imprison. Our court, presided over by wise old Jim Browning,[2] thought it desirable that each of us know first hand what trial was like. I thought so too, especially since I had never set foot inside a trial as a lawyer. Like the majority of lawyers in large firms, I had worked for corporate clients who eschewed litigation. I had occasionally had a case involving the appeal by an individual of a will or a trust, but that was a matter of marshaling legal rules. I had gone from the firm to teaching law at Notre Dame and then at Berkeley. I lacked experience in the give and take of lawyers in combat.

As a stimulus to our members to get trial judge experience, our court offered a month without appellate cases in exchange for a month of being a trial judge. A month off calendar as a judge of the court of appeals in exchange for a month on calendar as a district judge—the equation looks arithmetic. In fact, it was five days off from hearing appeals in exchange for four weeks of conducting trials. But the trade was not necessarily unfair. In those days, in the 1980's, the appeals court met for only five days a month. In those five days the court heard argument in 20 cases. Each case invariably had attached to it an opening brief, a reply brief, and a rebuttal brief, in all about 70 pages of printed matter. Each case had what was termed an "excerpt" of the trial record—sometimes one volume of 300 pages, sometimes six such volumes. Each case in short carried with it a mass of reading if you did nothing but read what the lawyers put before you. If you went outside the lawyers' presentation of the law and read relevant cases and treatises and law reviews yourself, you could add at least another 100 pages of reading. Not to mention that a law clerk would prepare a 15 to 30 page memo setting out an analysis of the case. And all this reading was merely preparatory to deciding the case. If you were assigned the job

2. James R. Browning (1918–2012) served on the Ninth Circuit from 1961 to 2012, assuming senior status in 2000. He was the circuit's chief judge (1976–1988) when John Noonan joined the court.

of writing the opinion explaining the decision, the writing could take from three hours to a week. So, five days off from appeals was relief from, maybe, a month or more of judicial labor.

In the district court, conducting a trial, your reading shrank greatly. Your rulings of law had to be made, generally speaking, from the bench on the spot. Occasionally, you could put off a ruling until after the lunch break or even overnight. But you didn't read a lot of law, and you didn't go through a massive record. The trial was creating the record. Usually, so I experienced, your nights were free. At least they were for me as I wrote no opinions. Four weeks of trial for five days of appeals wasn't a bad bargain.

District judges don't try many cases. Ten or twelve a year, I've heard them estimate. That is because cases settle before trial or get dismissed by the judge as failing even to state a possible case or are decided by summary judgment. Summary judgment was relatively new, a process I never heard about in law school. It requires a showing of facts by the party seeking it and the failure of the opposing party to refute those facts. Then the judge decides the case on the facts admitted. The process avoids trial by jury. It is relatively expeditious. It tempts district judges to find facts to be undisputed when there are actually disputes about them. On the whole, it's a time-saver as well as a life-saver for the judicial system. If every case had to go before a jury, the clogging would bring the system to a halt.

But why was I trying a man who'd learned his law in Quincy, Massachusetts? I was a judge of the Ninth Circuit with a home base in San Francisco and a home in Berkeley. The answer is I wanted the trial experience but didn't look forward to having my initial efforts as a trial judge reviewed by my colleagues on the circuit. In addition, my father was ill, so I had an excuse to go to Boston, an excuse necessary to get the approval of the committee on intercircuit transfers.

Once back in Boston, I was to discover, I was at home in a way that I never was in California. Until I was thirty-four, I had lived in Brookline, Massachusetts with only occasional breaks for the different worlds of Cambridge, Massachusetts; Cambridge, England; and Washington, D.C. In court in Boston, I knew where the litigants and the lawyers were coming from as I didn't know the backgrounds of those before me who came from any one of the nine western states that composed the Ninth Circuit. In Boston, I was attuned not to every note or nuance, but sensible of familiar patterns and capable of imagining the environments from which the litigants emerged.

My first case was, nonetheless, a shock. A tax protester! A tax protester representing himself without a lawyer—in the lexicon of the profession a pro se! A litigant without a lawyer is not a judge's dream. It may well be a judge's nightmare. What was the federal district court in Boston doing to me? Dumping on a visitor from California the dogs that no resident judge desired to try?

The first move of the electrician did nothing to reassure me. He asked me to issue a subpoena summoning the District Director of Internal Revenue to testify at the trial. The relevance of what the District Director might have to contribute was not obvious. What was obvious was that a subpoena would have generated inconvenience for the tax people. I denied the request.

A trial is not a play. Still less is it a painting. But like a role or a painting a frame provides a setting that brings critical elements into relation with each other and sets them apart from other elements. There is art in the conduct of a trial, although the judge is not a sole conductor but normally shares the baton with two opposing lawyers. Together, court and counsel, observing formal rules, create what is more than a tableau vivant. Their creation is life-focused, dramatized, brought to some sort of intermediate conclusion. If the play's the thing to catch the conscience of the king, a trial that ends in the judgment of a living person must test the conscience of each participant.

After the initial skirmish, the electrician was a well-mannered litigator. He politely cross-examined the government witness, who said that he had not filed. In his own defense, he swore himself in as a witness and elicited from himself the testimony that, according to the Constitution, he had no obligation to file. An assistant United States attorney, a bright young woman, told the jury that he was mistaken. He maintained that he had obeyed the Constitution. The trial was over in less than two days. I then had to instruct the jury on the law.

I'd brought with me one law clerk, Doug Blakeman. With his research confirming mine, I had come to the curious conclusion that there were two federal laws either one of which might apply to the case. One was the law the government had chosen to call upon when it charged the electrician with a crime. This law stamped failure to file as a felony. The crime was to be punished by imprisonment up to five years and a fine up to $100,000, or both. The other law treated failure to file as less than a felony, as a misdemeanor. The crime could still be punished by prison or a fine, but it was measurably less serious—not exactly like spitting on the sidewalk but not exactly like defrauding the government. I determined that the jury should be told of the alternatives.

There was another wrinkle, one gropingly reached for by the pro se as he recited his belief in the force of the Fourth and Fifth Amendments. A complete defense to the crime described by either statute was good faith. Good faith is one of the chameleon phrases of the law, popping up everywhere from contract law to copyright law. In this particular context of the criminal law, good faith meant the belief that one's conduct was innocent. If the jury believed the defendant's account of his activities, he should be acquitted.

To this effect I instructed the jury, noting also that if the jury did not believe the defendant, it should decide whether his offense was a felony or a misdemeanor, and adding that the jury should not reach a compromise: he was either guilty or not, and if guilty, of one offense and not the other. I was a bit taken aback when the prosecutor approached the bench and said to me in a low voice, "I didn't think you would give the closing argument for the defense." Free speech flourishes in Boston, I thought to myself.

The jury then retired to deliberate. The jury room was adjacent to the robing room where I removed the black garment that, like the elevated chair I sat in, served to give physical identification to my role as the judge. I could hear the noises from the jury room, not distinct words but the level and temperature of discourse. The jurors were shouting at each other. I imagined what they were saying: "He's innocent. He was sincere. He believed what he was saying, what he read in the Constitution." "You're crazy or stupid or naive. No one could believe that. Everybody's got to pay their taxes." Five o'clock came. The jury had not reached a verdict and went home.

The next morning the impasse continued. I considered giving them an instruction known as the *Allen* charge from the case where it was approved.[3] The *Allen* charge is sometimes referred to as dynamite interjected into jury deliberations. But its message is mild. It simply tells the jury that the case before it has to be decided; that it is not likely that

3. *Allen v. United States*, 164 U.S. 492 (1896).

another twelve men and women will be better able to decide it than the jury now in session; that they are not to decide against what they honestly have concluded and are not to compromise; and that they should try to reach a verdict. At 11:00 a.m., I gave the *Allen* charge. By noon, the jury returned a verdict: Guilty of the misdemeanor.

What did I think of the verdict? A sensible result. The defendant was not a felon as the community understands what felons are. Nor was he so unbelievably uninformed as to what everyone else took the law to be that he was innocent of any sense of wrongdoing. Was the verdict a compromise among the jurors? Probably, but it was not for me or anyone to ask. I entered the judgment of conviction.

Sentencing remained. The Sentencing Guidelines did not cover crimes committed before their enactment, so I was spared the necessity of looking at a chart like something in a board game. I was glad in this case not to have to follow them.[4] The punishment should fit the crime, be educative and rehabilitative and fit the person being sentenced. Sentencing is necessarily a subjective task.

In this case, I sentenced the electrician to probation and to paying what he owed with interest; to doing electrical work free for nonprofits for a few months; and to writing a book report on Tocqueville's *Democracy in America*. The trial was over. I hung up my robe and my role.

The electrician did not appeal. He performed his required labor for charity. He read Tocqueville and wrote a very decent book report. I thought I had seen the last of the case.

Nine months later, after I'd returned to California, I discovered that I was mistaken. He had not filed the federal income tax now due. He was still convinced that he didn't have to file. His probation officer noted that a standard condition of probation is not to commit a crime while you are on it. Breach of this condition is required for revocation of probation. As the sentencing judge, I was called to Boston to conduct a revocation-of-probation and resentencing hearing.

"This must be an important case," a lawyer remarked to me in the elevator in Boston, "if they bring you all the way from California to hear it." In the great flow of federal litigation, a revocation-of-probation hear-

4. Judge Noonan discussed his view of the Sentencing Guidelines again on 29–34, 37, 118.

ing is run-of-the-mill. But for the individual involved the case was important, and I found it important for me.

What was I going to do? Send to a federal prison for at least a year a person whose guideless gullibility to the tax protester doctrine seemed endless? What was accomplished by incarceration? Yet I had taken an oath to support the Constitution. The criminal law to be enforced had been enacted under the Constitution. I could not uphold the Constitution and fail to enforce the law.

I addressed the defendant in open court as a medieval inquisitor might have addressed a heretic. I pointed out to him that millions of his fellow citizens, hundreds of thousands of lawyers, thousands of judges did not share his idiosyncratic reading of the Constitution. He, poor heretic, was alone. Would not his wife and his two small children miss him? I would give him a week to think it over.

At the end of the week, he capitulated. He filed the return. The law had been upheld and had been obeyed. If the penalty had been death by fire at the stake instead of a year at Danbury, would I also have threatened to enforce it, and have enforced it, if the culprit had been recalcitrant or relapsed? I asked myself these questions but in the end saw no need to answer questions that were only mine.

TWO

# The Subversive Submissive[1]

I HAD SAT HEARING ARGUMENT in only one other session of the appeals court when I heard the case of Olimpia Lazo-Majano. Immigration law was a field foreign to my experience. I had never had an immigration case in private practice. I had never taught an immigration case in teaching Professional Responsibility. I was aware, however, that aliens as a class were treated differently from, and worse than, citizens. In that respect, a lawyer's responsibility to them was higher, for they were partially disabled to act for themselves, a point I had made in teaching Professional Responsibility using a case involving a lawyer for a slave in Alabama before the Civil War. I was familiar with the biblical injunction "You too must love the alien, for you once lived as aliens in Egypt" (Deut. 10:19), a passage read aloud at my installation as a judge. And I had the help of a law clerk, John Maguire, who held a doctorate in sociology from Berkeley where Robert Bellah had rated him as among the most brilliant students ever in the department. Maguire led me within the contours and around the crevices of the system governing the admission of aliens as refugees into the United States.

---

1. *Lazo-Majano v. INS*, 813 F.2d 1432 (9th Cir. 1987). *See also* John T. Noonan, Jr., *Lazo-Majano: Alive, Well, and Thriving at Twenty-Seven*, 28 Harv. Hum. Rts. J. 1 (2015). In *Fisher v. INS*, 79 F.3d 955, 963 (9th Cir. 1996), the Ninth Circuit sitting en banc overruled *Lazo-Majano* to the extent it could be understood to allow the court "to take judicial notice of information not part of the administrative record or not previously submitted to the Board" of Immigration Appeals. Judge Noonan dissented on the merits as well as on the question of judicial notice. *Id.* at 971–72 (Noonan, Cir. J., dissenting).

Olimpia, as I referred to her for humanity's sake in the opinion—what a travesty it is to refer to someone in her shoes as "petitioner," and what mock formality to call her Mrs. Lazo-Majano—was, in the formula used in such cases, "seeking review" of a decision of the Board of Immigration Appeals that had affirmed a decision of an immigration judge. A refugee from El Salvador, she had asked for the remedies offered by our law to a victim of persecution—the withholding of deportation or the grant of asylum. She had been denied both. If we granted her petition and sent the case back to the Board, it was highly likely that she would be granted relief.

Her story was unchallenged by the immigration service and assumed to be true by the immigration judge and the Board. It ran as follows: She was thirty-four, married, and the mother of three children. In 1981, when she was twenty-nine, her husband left El Salvador for political reasons: he had been in the rightist paramilitary group known as ORDEN; when he quit he was wanted by the guerrillas and distrusted by the government. Olimpia had always lived in the same small town. For five years she had been working as a domestic for another woman, getting a day off every fifteen days. In the middle of April 1982, she received a telephone call from Sergeant Rene Zuniga, who had known her since childhood. He asked her to wash his clothes. Olimpia agreed. On her day off during the next six weeks Olimpia worked for Zuniga at Zuniga's place. Zuniga then pointed out that Olimpia's husband was no longer in El Salvador and from this fact drew his conclusions. In Olimpia's words: "With a gun in his hand he made me be his."

In the following months Olimpia accepted Zuniga's domination. She continued to wash for him on her days off. She accepted taunts, threats, and beatings from him. He broke her identity card in pieces and forced her to eat the pieces. He dragged her by the hair about a public restaurant. He pummeled her face, causing a blood clot to form in one eye; she thought that she had lost the eye. She was nervous, preoccupied, and depressed, ate little, and became thin and frail. She wanted to escape her tormentor but saw no way of doing so.

Central to the situation was the fact that Zuniga was a sergeant in the Fuerza Armada, the Armed Force which is the Salvadoran military. Zuniga used his gun in forcing Olimpia to submit the first time. On another occasion Zuniga held two hand grenades against her forehead. On another occasion he threatened to bomb her. When he referred to her husband, Zuniga said that if he returned Zuniga himself would cut him apart, kill Olimpia as well, and say that they were both subversives. Zuniga informed Olimpia that it was his job to kill subversives.

Zuniga said to Olimpia that if she ever told on him he would have her tongue cut off, her nails removed one by one, her eyes pulled out, and she would then be killed. As Olimpia recalled his statement, he said: "And I can just say that you are contrary to us; subversive." When he was angry with her in the restaurant, he told a friend from the police "in front of all the other people in the restaurant" that she was a subversive and that was why her husband had left: "because she was a subversive."

Olimpia believed the Armed Force would let Zuniga carry out his threat. She believed that in 1979 a nineteen-year-old boy she knew by sight had been tied, tortured and killed by the Armed Force; that in 1981 the husband of a neighbor had been taken away in a truck at night with fifteen others and killed by the Armed Force; that the Armed Force had raped "young college girls," as had Zuniga himself. In her view there was nobody in El Salvador that could stop the Armed Force from doing such things. In her experience when Zuniga was dragging her by the hair in the restaurant no one helped because where the Armed Force was concerned, "no one will get involved."

That Zuniga's treatment of Olimpia constituted persecution was beyond dispute. Three questions remained, the first of which was, Had she not consented to his conduct? To that question an opinion in another case by Judge Harry Pregerson, a fellow panel member, provided a compelling answer.[2] Judge Pregerson had commented on the acquiescence of the victim of a kidnaping where the defendant had urged that her acquiescence absolved him of any crime. To the contrary, Judge Pregerson denied the defense and noted that her passivity presented a pattern, all too familiar, of a victim identifying with the aggressor under conditions of terror. She lacked "sufficient ego-strength, self-confidence and will-power" to escape or cry out for help.[3] So, too, Olimpia's identification with her persecutor did not transform the persecution into collaboration.

My analysis of Olimpia's conduct came perilously close to factfinding, an activity forbidden an appellate court. In my judgment, her psychology was implicit in her story. Accepting her account as fact, we accepted the psychology written on its face.

---

2. Harry Pregerson (1923–2017) was a district judge (1967–79) and served on the Ninth Circuit (1979–2015).

3. *United States v. Winters*, 729 F.2d 602, 605 (9th Cir. 1984).

The second question was, Were Zuniga's acts those of the government? Our law attributes to a government those acts that the government is unable or unwilling to restrain.[4] I thought it evident that Zuniga had impunity to do what he wanted with Olimpia. He acted as a member of the Armed Force, a military power that exercised domination over much of El Salvador despite the staunchest efforts of the Duarte government to restrain it. Zuniga had his gun, his grenades, his bombs, his authority and his hold over Olimpia because he was a member of this powerful military group that the government lacked power to control.

The third question was the most difficult. Were Zuniga's acts on account of Olimpia's political opinion? His conduct, the government argued, was deplorable but personal, a sado-masochistic relation between two "sweethearts." To this not implausible contention, the most obvious answer was that he had maintained his hold over her by attributing to her a political opinion. She would be killed as a subversive, Zuniga had told her, if she complained about him. She was a subversive, Zuniga had told a restaurant.

In immigration law, it is the belief that the persecutor attributes to his victim that counts. The victim herself can be innocent of any political beliefs. If the persecutor treats her as the enemy of the country, the victim is subject to persecution on account of the political opinion assigned by the persecutor: so, in an earlier case, a citizen of Tito's Yugoslavia, unwilling to become an informer for the secret police, had been labeled as a subversive by the police and, being persecuted by them, became entitled to asylum.[5] The fact that Zuniga gave Olimpia the choice of being subjected to physical injury and rape or being killed as a subversive did not alter the significance of the political opinion he attributed to Olimpia. Because of that attribution, Olimpia had to suffer the series of indignities that everyone saw as persecution.

In answering these three questions I concluded that Olimpia met the criteria for relief. In my opinion I went further than was necessary to specify a second political opinion on whose account Olimpia feared fu-

4. *See, e.g.*, *Sarvia-Quintanilla v. U.S. INS*, 767 F.2d 1387, 1391 n. 1 (9th Cir. 1985) (section 243(h) of the Immigration and Naturalization Act forbids the deportation of a noncitizen who shows, among other facts, "a likelihood of persecution [and] that the source of the likely persecution is either the government of his country or a group that the government is unable or unwilling to control").

5. *Kovac v. INS.*, 407 F.2d 102 (9th Cir. 1969).

ture persecution. If the situation was seen in its social context, Zuniga was asserting the political opinion that a man has a right to dominate women. He had persecuted Olimpia to force her to accept this opinion without rebellion. Zuniga told Olimpia that in his treatment of her he was seeking revenge. But Olimpia knew of no injury she had ever done Zuniga. His statement reflected a much more generalized animosity to the opposite sex, an assertion of a political aspiration and the desire to suppress opposition to it. Olimpia was not permitted by Zuniga to hold an opinion to the contrary. When by flight, she asserted one, she became exposed to persecution for her assertion. Future persecution threatened her because of this political opinion. This probability of future political persecution was a second, independent reason for granting relief.

Under one statute, an alien was entitled to withholding of deportation if it was more likely than not that she would be persecuted on account of her political opinion if deported to her native land. That meant there had to be a 51% chance of persecution. Under a second statute an alien was entitled to asylum, in the discretion of the Attorney General, if she had "a well-founded fear of persecution" on account of her political opinion. To meet this discretionary standard, the chances had to be one in ten. We held that the Board, to whom the Attorney General's discretion had been delegated, had abused that discretion in denying her asylum and that the Board's decision denying withholding of deportation was not supported by substantial evidence. The chances were one in ten, even more than five in ten, that she would suffer at Zuniga's hands, if sent back.[6]

---

6. In his dissent in *Fisher v. INS* (see n. 1 above), Noonan summarized his view of that case:

> we are asked in this en banc court to decide whether the Board had substantial evidence for concluding that Saideh Hassib-Tehrani had fear, and reason to fear, persecution on account of her religious beliefs and political opinion if she were now deported to Iran. In the end, in deciding that question we are required to integrate the objective evidence with her subjective emotions and to ask whether a person with her experiences, who fell ill after being handcuffed and detained for four hours, would be scared of suffering on account of her now openly expressed opposition to the regime if she were sent back. In *Bastanipour,* Judge Posner asked the government's lawyer "whether *he* would fear persecution by Iran if he were in Bastanipour's religious and political shoes and he conceded that he would." *Bastanipour v. INS*, 980 F.2d 1129, 1133 (7th Cir. 1992). We did not ask the government lawyer a similar question but we should ask ourselves: If we had the beliefs and

Judge Pregerson was the other judge constituting that "we" issuing this opinion. Our colleague, Cecil Poole, dissented[7]. He wrote:

> The record here shows a Salvadoran woman, Lazo-Majano, who was abused and dominated by an individual purely for sexual, and clearly ego reasons. Neither petitioner nor her tormentor was "politically" motivated in any sense contemplated by the laws granting asylum to aliens. The holding that, as a matter of law, Lazo-Majano was persecuted on account of political opinion, is a construct of pure fiction.

Judge Poole took special umbrage at our view of the political nature of the future persecution that Olimpia feared. He wrote:

> Quite simply, the majority has outdone Lewis Carroll in its application of the term "political opinion" and in finding that male domination in such a personal relationship constitutes political persecution.

Judge Poole did not think Zuniga's threats to treat Olimpia as a subversive were credible. The threats "were effective because she was unsophisticated enough to believe that this low-grade bully-tyrant might make trouble." Judge Poole did not acknowledge that Zuniga appeared to be unrestrained by the government of El Salvador. For him, the relationship between Zuniga and Olimpia was not political but personal.

Given this spirited dissent, it was not surprising that the government sought rehearing by the panel and rehearing en banc by the court. We

---

> the experience and the gender of Saideh Hassib-Tehrani, would we reasonably fear that we had a one-in-ten chance of suffering seriously on account of our beliefs if we returned to Iran? The answer, it may be suggested, is obvious. If it is obvious, the Board necessarily erred in its contrary finding.

*Fisher*, 79 F.3d at 971–72 (Noonan, Cir. J., dissenting) (citation completed). Noonan's views on a great many issues could hardly have more unlike those of Richard Posner, who left the University of Chicago law faculty to serve on the Seventh Circuit from 1981 to 2017 (chief judge 1993–2000). But Noonan recognized Posner's stature as a judge. *See* below, page 56, where Noonan describes Posner as "the most brilliant of academics on the federal bench." *See also* Richard A. Posner, *Reply to Critics of the Problematics of Moral and Legal Theory*, 111 Harv. L. Rev. 1796, 1796 (1998) (identifying Noonan as one of the two "most distinguished living judges who, before ascending the bench, made important contributions as academics to both jurisprudence and moral theory").

7. Cecil F. Poole (1914–97) served as a district judge (1976–80), and on the Ninth Circuit (1979–97). (Poole continued to sit in district court cases for several months after receiving his commission as a circuit judge.)

had, we were informed by the government's petition, "transmogrified" immigration law by our view that machismo could constitute a political opinion whose assertion would be political. "Transmogrify" is a word that sounds formidable but whose meaning is unknown to most who hear it. Webster's says the word means "to change in form, appearance or structure, often with grotesque or humorous effect." I assumed that the government was contending that our effect was grotesque. We denied the petition. No judge asked for rehearing en banc. Certiorari was not sought. The central holding remains the law that the political opinion the persecutor attributes to his victim is decisive in determining on what account the asylum-seeker has been persecuted.

THREE

# Three Options for an Asylum-Seeker[1]

THE THREE OPTIONS OF JESUS ESCOBAR-GRIJALVA are best understood as put to her by the immigration judge hearing her case. A little context needs to be supplied.

The options and the context are captured in the following, an excerpt from the stenographic transcription of the hearing:

## JUDGE FOR THE RECORD

This is a continued proceeding at Los Angeles, California on October 24, 1996, in deportation proceedings in the matter of Jesus Escobar-Grijalva, A 72 519 396. On behalf of the respondent, no attorney or representative has appeared. And on behalf of the Service, general attorney Mr. Alan Youtsler. The official Spanish interpreter and court clerk is Sinyova (phonetic sp.) Lopez.

## JUDGE TO MS. ESCOBAR

Q To the respondent, Ms. Escobar, it is now five after two, over an hour—

A Oh, wait, wait, Your Honor. I apologize.

Q Oh, thank you. Over an hour past the scheduled time that your case was scheduled for a hearing. We have waited your attorney.[2] That is, at the last hearing—well, previous hearings you have had

1. *Escobar-Grijalva v. INS*, 206 F.3d 1331 (9th Cir.).
2. Thus in the manuscript and in the opinion.

various attorneys, Mr. Davis, Ms. McGuire, Ms. Scott, and you continue apparently to be represented by attorneys from that office. Who is your present attorney, because no one is with you?

A It's a new American one.

Q A new American one? What is the name of this attorney?

A I don't know.

Q Well, where is he, ma'am? I mean, you were sitting here and your attorney's not here.

A (Indiscernible). He told me that he was already here. But I didn't see him.

Q Have you even met this new attorney, yet, ma'am? This new American attorney as you described him to be?

A Yes, I saw him.

Q What is the name of this attorney? It looks like Jeremy Frost is his name. Is that his name?

A (Indiscernible).

Q A man, according to the writing in here, at least. He is still part of the same law office of McGuire and company. But, my question to you, ma'am, is where is any of your attorneys? Where are they?

A I don't know, it—can you allow me to go out and see.

Q Well, ma'am, have you seen them today at all? Any of your attorneys?

A Yes, I did see him.

Q You saw Mr. Frost?

A Yes.

Q Or was this gentleman his assistant that you saw, ma'am? Don't get the two confused.

A No, it (indiscernible).

Q Okay, and he said he would be representing you? When did you last see him? When did you last see him ma'am?

A I just saw him before I got in here. Would you please allow me to go out one moment.

Q We'll have the court interpreter go out there and call his name.

*(off the record)*

*(on the record)*

JUDGE FOR THE RECORD

Back on the record. Off the record, the court interpreter would [list] the respondent's witness.

JUDGE TO MR. FROST

Q Counsel, I understand you're Jeremy Frost, is that right?

A That's correct, Your Honor.

JUDGE TO MS. ESCOBAR

Q Now, ma'am, is this your attorney, Mr. Frost?

A No.

Q No?

A It's another one.

JUDGE TO MR. FROST

Q Okay, well, counsel, have you ever met your client?

A No, I haven't, Your Honor. But I'm—I'm from—

[MS. ESCOBAR TO JUDGE]

A He hasn't seen me.

JUDGE TO THE INTERPRETER

Q Wait, wait. Let—let her finish. What—what's that?

A He—it's another gentleman.

Q Okay, well, Mr. Frost is from the law offices of Terance McGuire. He is one apparently one of the new attorneys.

A Actually—

Q This is not the person you—you met outside? The new attorney you said—the new American attorney?

A With a black jacket.

### JUDGE TO MR. FROST

Q Counsel, do you have any idea who that is?

A No, I don't, Your Honor.

Q Is that one of your assistants maybe? One of your clerks or something?

A I'm—I'm not even with McGuire's office. I'm with Jim Valanti (phonetic sp.)—Valinoti.

Q You're with Valinoti? Well—

A Yeah.

Q (indiscernible) really confusing me, because your—your notice comes in—in McGuire's office's name, not Valinoti's. And is there some reason why you submitted a notice with another law firm? I mean, I'm really confused now. If you're with Mr. Valinoti's office, why are you submitting a notice under Mr. Terance McGuire's offices?

A Your Honor, I'm a little confused too. And if I could call a recess for five minutes to just get it clarified. I—I really don't have the answer.

Q Have you met your client before today, counsel. I mean, right now, because she said she never saw you before until you walked in right now.

A That's true, Your Honor. I've never met her.

Q And you're going to be presenting her case?

A Actually, I was hoping to have time, you know, before, but I just ran from this hearing to this hearing.

### MR. YOUTSLER [COUNSEL FOR THE GOVERNMENT] TO JUDGE

Q I don't think he can represent her. He hasn't ever met her before. He has no idea what her case [is] about.

### JUDGE TO MR. FROST

Q Yeah, counsel, I—at the minimum I'm a little concerned. First of all, whose law firm are you associated with?

A Jim Valinoti, Your Honor.

Q Jim Valinoti? Okay, so you're not associated with McGuire, Scott and Company?

A No, Your Honor. But if I get a chance to talk with Jim, maybe I could get some clarification into who is actually handling this file.

Q No, counsel. I'm going to ask the respondent what she wants.

A Okay

## JUDGE TO MS. ESCOBAR

Q Ma'am, do you want this gentleman to represent you?

A Those are my papers, but if the man is not here—

Q Well, ma'am, let me tell you, I want to make sure you understand something. You're going to have basically three choices. And let me explain to you what they are. You're going to have the choice, number 1, of choosing this gentleman who claims he represents you, although never meeting you today yet, to represent and present your case today. Or, you have the choice of proceeding on your own and being your own attorney and representing yourself today and presenting your case. That's the second choice. Or, the third choice is, I will give you a continuance to get a new attorney to represent you. And when I say that, ma'am, if you get a new attorney, it's not going to be any of the following people. And I will not allow them to appear. And that includes Mr. Frost, Mr. McGuire, Mr. Alexander, Ms. Scott or Mr. Davis or Mr. Valinoti or Mr. Cassarian (phonetic sp.). None of those people. Because you see, supposedly this gentleman represents all of them as one of their attorneys. And I'm not about to continue a case for some—one of them from the same law offices to walk in when they should have been ready today to present your case. So if you don't accept Mr. Frost from these law firms, none of those individuals will be representing you at your next hearing. Now if you get a new attorney unrelated to any of them, I don't have a problem. You're more than welcome to do that. But I'm not having one of those attorneys from the same law offices walk in and get a delay because they don't know what's going on with their cases. They're not going to get that continuance for that purpose. They're going to be removed as your attorney, and they're not going to represent you. So, ma'am, of those three choices, what would you like? Mr. Frost to present your case today? You to do it on your own? Or, you can find a new attorney completely separate and apart from any of these attorneys I've mentioned (indiscernible) who have filed notices with me.

A It's okay. If he doesn't miss again, he doesn't, you know, show up again.

Q So you want Mr. Frost to represent you? Is that what you said? Choice number 1?

A I don't know what he said.

Q That's what I don't know, ma'am. Is that choice number 1 you're selecting?

A It's okay.

Q That's fine, ma'am. We're going to proceed then.

The reader will have noted that there are a few non sequiturs or gaps in the transcript, perhaps due to failures by the translator or the stenographer, but that, on the whole, the non sequiturs follow from the immigration judge pursuing his own train of thought without paying too much attention to Alan Youtsler, Jeremy Frost, or Jesus Escobar-Grijalva, usually referred to by him as "the respondent." The immigration judge has business to be done. He must get through a crowded calendar. He is tired of immigration attorneys shuffling cases and clients, imposing on immigration judges and on hapless petitioners. So in the case of Jesus Escobar-Grijalva the immigration judge imposed order, and Jeremy Frost conducted an examination of her, eliciting the story of her reasons for leaving Guatemala and for fearing to return there.

At the end of the hearing, the immigration judge denied Jesus Escobar-Grijalva's petition. The Board of Immigration Appeals affirmed this decision. She then appealed to this court.

The first question I had to answer was whether Jesus Escobar-Grijalva had been denied the help of a lawyer. She had no constitutional right to a lawyer. The Sixth Amendment to the Constitution gives that right only to a defendant in "criminal proceedings." Immigration hearings are not considered to be "criminal proceedings," even though deportation may be as drastic a penalty for the immigrant as many criminal sentences.

But in 1952, the House Judiciary Committee under Congressman Emanuel Celler reported an immigration reform bill that the committee stated gave an alien "the right of being represented (at no expense to the Government) by counsel." The bill became law with this section of the statute carrying the heading "The Right to Counsel." The actual wording of the statute was nuanced. It declared that the alien had "the privilege" of being represented by counsel. The softening of "right" to "privilege" took account of the provision that the government could not be made to pay for the alien's lawyer, but did not turn the statute into a mere recommendation that the alien be allowed counsel. A privilege granted by statute is a species of right. A privilege, if asserted, must be enforced. Jesus Escobar-Grijavlva at her hearing was asserting her privilege.

Like many phrases used in law, the phrase "represented by counsel" has a breadth of meaning and evokes a history beyond the three words employed. Here what is evoked is what it means to have as an advocate one professionally skilled in the subject. Does it mean being represented by someone you have just met, who is familiar with the pattern of questions in immigration cases but knows nothing of the particular strengths and weaknesses of your case? Such a person, who has gone to law school and been admitted to the bar and knows how to ask routine questions, is certainly a lawyer. No one familiar with the history and standards of the legal profession would think of him as an advocate. No one immersed in the ethos of our profession would credit such a scarecrow with being counsel representing a client.

Alexander Solzhenitsyn in his account of life in the Soviet Union has a passage on the precious privilege of counsel, of having, at a moment of great trial in one's life, "a clear-minded ally who knows the law."[3] Was Jeremy Frost such a clear-minded ally for Jesus Escobar-Grijalva because Frost knew the law and could articulate questions in terms of it? By no means, for nothing suggests that Frost was her ally. He had wandered, for some unexplained purpose, into the hearing. He was not connected with the McGuire firm that the immigration judge believed he belonged to. He was, as it were, press-ganged into appearing for this woman he had never met. Is it necessary to say that even in a totalitarian dictatorship Jeremy Frost would not have appeared as the ally of the person facing expulsion from the country?

---

3. *The Gulag Archipelago: 1918–1956*, at 56 (HarperCollins 2002) (1973).

*Res ipsa loquitur*—"the thing itself speaks," a Latin maxim of English tort law, is useful in a variety of contexts. So the transcript of this hearing spoke to me. The hearing was a mess, with misunderstandings just short of a situation on Saturday Night Live. Granting the immigration judge an honest purpose and an harassed schedule, he had forced Frost on Escobar. Even if her, "It's okay" could be read as acquiescence, it was a consent coerced out of her as she was offered options, none of them acceptable. "I don't know what he said" appears to be her summation of what the immigration judge presented.

On these facts, speaking as they seemed to me, it was easy to conclude that Jesus Escobar-Grijalva had been denied the effective assistance of counsel, her statutory privilege had been violated, and the case must be remanded for a new hearing. One member of our three-judge panel dissented, writing, "To have the privilege of being represented is not to have a right to counsel that the state must enforce." But if a court did not enforce the privilege what meaning would it have? An unenforceable privilege is empty talk. Congress, I had no doubt, had committed itself to a fair process.[4]

---

4. *See also* John T. Noonan, Jr., *Immigration Law 2006*, 55 Cath. U. L. Rev. 905, 909–10 (2006):

Such was the record in this case where at issue was Jesus Escobar's asylum in the United States—a series of false starts, of non sequiturs, of unanswered questions, of misunderstood answers, culminating, despite government counsel's intelligent intervention, in the immigrant being saddled by the judge with a lawyer who had never seen her before. It's hard to pin all the fault here on any single person. Was it the interpreter who didn't get everything said? Was it the stenographer, who probably wasn't there but sometime later listened to the taped recording of the proceeding and did her best to render it intelligible? Was it the immigration judge, who so often seems to follow his own train of thought without paying much attention to government counsel, to Jeremy Frost, or to Ms. Escobar herself?

However the blame is to be assigned for a jumble that comes close to a skit on *Saturday Night Live*, imagine coming to a court of law with this transcript! A panel of the Board made its decision based on this record. Lawyers in the Justice Department then chose to defend the Board's decision in the court of appeals. The government did not concede error and ask for a remand. Speaking now from my point of view, it was mulish persistence in defending a decision based on this record that constituted the capital mistake made in this asylum case.

FOUR

# An Aberrant Act[1]

AKIKO MAGNESON MET THE AGENT on the flight home from Tokyo. They were seatmates and became chatty. The agent told her he worked for the government, for the immigration service in fact. She'd been an immigrant herself, from Yokohama, and was naturally interested. She was also an importer, running a small business in gems out of her home and thinking about importing cloth from Bangkok. She could have problems with red tape. As they parted in San Francisco at the end of their long flight, he told her, "If there's anything I can do for you, just give me a call."

A month later Akiko called the agent at the number on his card, a number at the offices of the immigration service in Washington. She recalled their trip and spoke in pleasantries, which the agent reciprocated. The agent sensed that the palaver was preliminary. Japanese would not plunge into business at once. The agent arranged to have his telephone bugged.

A few days later, Akiko called again. A friend of hers, Hiroyusu Takai, needed a green card for his just-married Japanese wife.

| | |
|---|---|
| Akiko | So many people have trouble and they pay. Why must they pay the lawyer? They pay cash, and you know, oh, you make money. |
| The agent | Yeah, I imagine there's a lot of, there must be a lot of money involved in something like that. |

1. *United States v. Takai*, 930 F.2d 1427 (9th Cir.), *amended*, 941 F.2d 738 (9th Cir. 1991).

| | |
|---|---|
| Akiko | Oh, yeah. |
| The agent | How many, how many people do you know? |
| Akiko | So many people." |
| The agent | How could I get to know these people? |
| Akiko | I can get the people, no trouble. |
| The agent | Well, we should talk. |
| Akiko | Any time if you want extra money, you know just tell me. I will not charge. I will not make money. You make money on it. I just give a name. |

The next day she called again. "I talked to several people." She needed green cards for four persons: Takai's wife, who was not "officially married" to him; two young boys who worked for Takai at his aviation school; and a Japanese friend of hers who was about to get a divorce. The agent observed that he had to be careful "more or less." Akiko: "Oh, I know very much, yes." They talked further about Takai's bride. The agent: "Okay, what is he more or less willing to do for me?" She: "$15,000." He: "For each of them?" She: "No, no. All together. Too small?" He said it was okay, but inquired whether there would be more people interested in doing this, "because I am at tremendous risk, you understand that."

The following day, Akiko called and put Takai on the line. The agent asked for $7,500 as a down payment. Takai: "No problem." He added that he would pay for the agent's ticket to San Francisco. In a subsequent call, the agent told Takai that the $7,500 would have to be in cash. "I don't want any record of a check or anything." Five days later, Takai telephoned the agent that he couldn't sleep for worry and that he was backing out. The agent then called Akiko, who observed that Takai "did scare." Akiko was ready to go ahead.

The very next day, the agent arrived in California and called Akiko from the Red Lion in San Jose. He gave his room number. She came with the cash and handed it to him. Their conversation was recorded. At the end of it, Akiko was arrested.

Takai and Akiko were indicted for bribing an official of the immigration service and for conspiracy to bribe him. Takai had backed out of paying money for himself but had loaned $1,500 to one of his employees for part of his bribe and had passed on to Akiko the bribe money from both boys. He pleaded guilty to the charges. So did Akiko. Like the great majority of federally indicted defendants, they were in fact guilty. As in the great majority of federal criminal cases, the argument centered on their sentencing.

For most of American history, the sentence has depended on the judge. In the 1970's and 80's, dissatisfaction with the judge had grown. In particular as to the federal system, some critics thought federal judges were too severe in their treatment of minorities. Others thought that they were not severe enough as to white collar criminals. Although the system enforced national legislation, sentencing for the same crime was not uniform throughout the nation. The differing ideological currents that coalesced to sponsor change were symbolized by Teddy Kennedy and Strom Thurmond being among the joint sponsors of a bill that altered the way sentencing was done for crimes committed after November 1, 1987.[2] In 2005, the Supreme Court pronounced part of the new system to be unconstitutional.[3] Most of my experience as an appellate judge has been with the system in force from 1987 to date, although fortunately, when I sat as a trial judge, I held trials only of pre-1987 crimes and was not constrained by what came into being in 1987 as the Sentencing Guidelines.

The Sentencing Guidelines bore a striking resemblance to the rules of a complicated board game and appropriately, therefore, culminated in a number of points which determined the defendant's sentence. The more points, the higher the sentence. Points were assigned to the crime itself—for example, 93 for first-degree murder, 12 for manslaughter by criminal negligence. To these points were added points for the defendant's criminal history—for example, 3 for each prior sentence of imprisonment over one year and one month. Points were added if the victim was especially vulnerable. Points were added depending on whether the role of the defendant was as an organizer or leader or manager. Points were subtracted if the role was "minor," and more were subtracted if the role was "minimal"—subtractions curiously captioned "Mitigating

---

2. The Sentencing Reform Act of 1984 created the United States Sentencing Commission and tasked it with drafting and promulgating federal Sentencing Guidelines, and with the Guidelines' ongoing interpretation and revision.

3. *United States v. Booker*, 543 U.S. 220 (2005), held that the provision of the Sentencing Reform Act that made conformity to the Sentencing Guidelines mandatory violated the Sixth Amendment. Since *Booker*, the Guidelines are only advisory, but they remain "the starting point and the initial benchmark" in federal sentencing. *Gall v. United States*, 552 U.S. 38, 49 (2007).

Role." Points were added for "obstructing justice," as by altering or destroying evidence, but not for committing perjury during the trial. Points were subtracted for accepting responsibility for the crime. The complexity of computation when multiple counts were charged is such that I abstain from summarizing the calculation. Nor can I possibly do justice to all the permutations and definitional quirks that affected the application of the rules.

Suffice it to say that so much detail was spelled out and so coercive was its content that it was apparent on their face that these rules were not optional "guidelines" as euphemistically described but authoritative directions that were meant to be enforced by the courts. Once all the points were tabulated, the judge was to turn to the Sentencing Table where the judge would find the sentences required by the points. These sentences were specified in terms of months—another kind of euphemism because 210 months seems less harsh than 17½ years. The sentences also always were in terms of a range of months, say 210–262, giving a residual bow to a judicial discretion dominated by the points. An antiseptic tone was preserved by this austere array of numbers.

As a further check on judges, the Guidelines had a laconic statement on race, sex, national origin, creed, religion and socio-economic status: "these factors are not relevant in the determination of a sentence." Age, education, mental condition, emotional condition, physical condition, past employment, prior good works, and family ties and responsibilities were all declared to be "not ordinarily relevant" either in deciding within the sentencing range dictated by the points or in departing from this range. With this thoughtful enumeration, many markers that might have eased a sentence, or sometimes increased it, were excluded.

The authors of the Sentencing Guidelines announced in an introduction that they had faced "a philosophical problem." The problem was the purpose of criminal punishment. Some thought the purpose to be "crime control," either by incapacitating the offender or deterring others. Some thought the purpose to be "just desserts," punishment proportionate to the offender's culpability and the harm caused. The authors did not choose between these purposes "because in most sentencing decisions the application of either philosophy will produce the same or similar results." Not documenting this claim, the authors went on to take "an empirical approach," meaning by that phrase that they tried to follow the past practice of the federal courts, depending on a variety of sources to estimate what that practice had been and sometimes not following it for "important reasons."[4] They created a manual of punishment over four hundred pages long.

In the following years this intricate scheme was annotated by appellate opinions in thousands of court cases. Given the complexity of the system and the continuing play of precedent upon it, nothing was easier to appeal in a criminal case than the sentence. The work of the criminal defense bar was largely displaced from the trial to the sentence. The government could not appeal an acquittal; it could appeal a sentence and now had at hand in the Sentencing Guidelines a set of rules to invoke for its appeal, so the government also began to litigate sentences.

Whether this massive effort to rationalize punishments was good or bad was hard for a federal judge to be sure. Since in 2005, after 17 years, part of the machine was stamped as defective, constitutionally, it was scarcely all good. It did seem better than the past practice described to me by a parole officer in Boston, who said that in the old days a judge would say, "Give me a number," and the parole officer would respond with the number of years he believed the crime called for. But there is much in the points and chart of the Sentencing Guidelines that seems pseudo-scientific, furnishing a certainty for a sentence for which no sure basis exists. And because points are the currency of the system, the system does have a game-like quality inappropriate in the disposition of human beings. I don't believe that a hospital that made its initial diagnosis on a point system would work well with the variety of patients treated. I do think that the sentence must fit both the crime and the criminal.[5]

---

4. https://www.ussc.gov/guidelines/2018-guidelines-manual/2018-chapter-1.

5. "Making the punishment fit the crime seems to be a purpose of the guidelines. It is the purpose so effectively satirized in Gilbert & Sullivan's *The Mikado*. Why is this worthwhile purpose open to satire? Because crimes are committed by human beings. The punishment should be appropriate for the crime. It should also fit the human person who committed the crime. The guidelines make this fit difficult." John T. Noonan, Jr., *The Guidelines have Distorted the System*, 5 Fed.Sent.R. 190, 190 (1993). *See also* John T. Noonan, Jr., *The Foxboro Referee, the Boston Judge, the County Juror, and the Conscience of the Court*, 2003 U. Ill. L. Rev. 1403, 1407 (2003):

> [C]onsider the United States Sentencing Guidelines (U.S.S.G.). We might add another S. to them and call them the United States Scientific Sentencing Guidelines. With their elaborate definitions and tables, they are a kind of parody of the scientific method. With their system of points and a massive rule book, they appear to be a giant board game. Yet they are not a science, for their tables predict nothing as to the future. They are not a game, for they bite into human lives in a way no game is allowed to do. The U.S.S.G. do confer a false objectivity onto a subjective decision.

In Akiko's case, ten points were assigned by the Guidelines for the crime of bribery. The crime of conspiracy to give a bribe was merged, for purposes of calculating the points, into the bribery itself. Three points were added because the bribe was over $10,000 and less than $20,000. Two points were subtracted because the defendants accepted responsibility. Their criminal history points were zero. With eleven points total, their sentences were set at between eight months to one year and two months. According to the Guidelines "at least one half of the minimum term" had to be "satisfied by imprisonment." Imprisonment, however, was not imposed by the judge in this case.

The judge was Robert E. Peckham.[6] Peckham had been appointed by President Nixon to the district court in 1966 and had served as its chief judge from 1976 to 1988. My impression of him from reading records on appeal from his decisions was that he would be described as "fair but tough" or as "tough but fair," depending on what the speaker sought to emphasize. In 1990, as he sentenced these defendants, he was sixty-nine years old, with twenty-four years' experience as a judge.

One facet of Judge Peckham's background I was unaware of at the time and came to know only in writing this chapter and seeking information about him on the Web. There I encountered a speech made in the House of Representatives by Congressman Norman Mineta in support of a bill to name the federal courthouse in San Jose after Judge Peckham. (The bill passed, and the courthouse is so named). Mineta, a leader in the community of Americans of Japanese heritage, spoke of the Peckhams as a family of lawyers and went on to note J.B. Peckham, the uncle of Judge Peckham. During World War II when the Japanese were expelled from California, many in the San Jose area conveyed their homes and businesses or farms to J.B. Peckham in trust, a trust which unlike certain scoundrels, he faithfully observed. "He was a legendary figure among Japanese Americans in my home town of San Jose," said Mineta.[7] I saw then how his nephew might have had ties or sympathies that influenced his judgment in our case, but also that he might have had a particularly sharpened sense of the kind of sentence that would do the

6. Robert F. Peckham (1920–93) was a California superior court judge (1959–66) and a federal district judge from 1966 to 1993.

7. *See* 139 Cong. Rec. 5205 (House) (remarks of Norman Y. Mineta, March 16, 1993).

most good in this community. Knowing about his uncle's status would, on balance, have given me confidence in his judgment.

Peckham sentenced each of the defendants to four months of house detention with special monitoring, fines of $15,000 apiece, and five years' probation. The monetary penalty was proportioned to what they had been willing to pay as a bribe. The restraint put on their liberty was limited. Probably the greatest penalty was the shame of their conviction. The sentences were merciful.

As the expression went, Judge Peckham had decided to depart downwards, as the statute permitted, for a "circumstance of a kind, or to a degree, not adequately taken into consideration by the Guidelines." Judge Peckham enumerated these circumstances. Neither Akiko nor Takai sought or received any financial reward for what they did. The government pointed to no other benefit they received. The agent of the immigration service had played "a pivotal role" in the crime, not enough of a role that they could present a defense of entrapment but enough of a role that his encouragement led them on. Their acts constituted "single acts of aberrant behavior."

All criminal behavior is aberrant, why should an act categorized as aberrant get a pass from prison? Is not the criminal act of a person who has ordinarily conducted herself with civil decorum worse than the crime of a person who has had trouble observing the law? Aren't isolated aberrant acts within the control of those committing them? These questions lingered in the background. Inferentially, the authors of the Sentencing Guidelines had found that judges did give a break to the ordinary law-abiding person mysteriously plunging into crime. It was not that her act had been uncontrollable or less controllable than that of a common criminal. It was a recognition that anyone can make a mistake, that sometimes the mistake is a crime, and that the full energies of criminal justice did not need to be deployed against anyone for a lapse that anyone might experience. As Dr. Samuel Johnson once put it, "A fallible person will fail sometimes."[8]

8. Judge Noonan was quoting from memory. Dr. Johnson's exact words, according to Boswell, were "Few have all kinds of merit belonging to their character. We must not examine matters too deeply—No, Sir, a *fallible being will fail somewhere.*" 2 James Boswell, *Life of Johnson* (1791), *Project Gutenberg* (2005, rev. 2014), https://www.gutenberg.org/cache/epub/9072/pg9072-images.html.

The government appealed. The United States Attorney in San Francisco regularly had one person in the office who specialized in criminal appeals and who for that reason was familiar not only with the law but with the characteristics of the judges. Unlike many courts, our court had so many members and covered so many thousands of miles that court and counsel in any given case were often unknown to each other. Rory K. Little, Assistant United States Attorney, did not have that disadvantage. He argued the appeal with sensitivity and with vigor.

The government's case began with two quotations from the Sentencing Commission, the agency created to promulgate the Sentencing Guidelines. The Commission had noted that pre-Guidelines, the courts had sentenced to probation "an inappropriately high percentage of offenders guilty of certain economic crimes." The Commission had also observed that "current sentencing practices do not adequately reflect the seriousness of public corruption offenses." Judge Peckham, the government now implied, had fallen back into an old pattern.

Addressing directly his reasons for departing downward, Little contended that the defendants would have benefitted from their bribery. They would have gained prestige in their immigrant community. Their businesses would have indirectly benefitted. As to the agent's part in encouraging the crime, if that were accepted as a valid reason for departure it would justify departure "in virtually every undercover case" (every being underscored). Finally, "single acts of aberrant behavior" constituted a ground "so vague that if endorsed by this court here, it will become the departure reason that swallows every white collar first-offense case."

Each one of these arguments resonated with me. They were not overstatements. The benefits suggested were probable if not certain. The practice of undercover agents playing along with a criminal was standard procedure, and undercover work of this kind seemed to be a necessary police technique. It was evident that what made the conduct here appear to be aberrant was that neither defendant had a criminal history. But that circumstance in itself did not excuse them from imprisonment.

I added to these arguments my own view of public corruption and its consequences. I had encountered the phenomenon in Massachusetts as the chairman of the Brookline Redevelopment Authority[9] where a redevelopment program was delayed for several years by the necessity of rid-

9. 1958–62.

ding it of corrupt interference. I had later written *Bribes*, a history of the slow acceptance of the difficult concept that there is something wrong in the subversion by money of a government officer's honest judgment.[10] I was aware of how lethargic some portions of the public were about such corruption. I was also aware of the current cant about victimless crimes. The bribe in the case we were reviewing had no victim. Honest government would have been damaged if the bribe had had an effect, but no person would have been injured. Absence of a victim did not make me think the crime more excusable. I took bribery as proof of the fallacy that required victims if an act were to be defined as criminal.

In their argument to us, Akiko and Takai went in the direction of a cultural defense, suggesting that they had naively stumbled into conduct that they did not know was criminal. In the face of the tapes of their telephone calls it was impossible to credit this suggestion. Both of them had been made aware that their plan was illegal. Why else was Takai scared?

Not innocent in intent, not so naive as to believe it legal, conspiring to gather recruits and to raise the cash, Akiko and Takai were not obvious candidates for compassion. What was on the other side? To begin with, there was the reasoned judgment of Judge Peckham himself. A number of rules are intended to establish different levels of scrutiny of the work of trial judges by appellate judges. These rules are beloved by some judges and by more law clerks. The rules are ready for mechanical application or manipulation. My first rule is to look at who the trial judge was. Judge Peckham's judgment deserved a large degree of deference. Add that he had heard and seen the defendants. Deciding whether to imprison people without seeing them is not, in my view, a desirable practice. But courts of appeals do not make arrangements to see criminal defendants. Lacking a look, I incline to accept the decision of the judge who did see them, especially if the judge has found a way not to imprison them.

Secondly, there were the views of my colleagues on the panel hearing the appeal. Tom Tang was from Phoenix, aged 73, fourteen years on the court, mild, courteous and kind, the son of an immigrant and the first person of Chinese ancestry to be appointed to our court on a coast so

---

10. Published in 1984.

favored by immigrants from Asia.[11] Six years earlier, Judge Tang had concurred in affirming a judgment of the conviction of a couple named Chen who had bribed an immigration officer to stay away from their restaurant where illegal immigrants were working. He wrote: "The government has won a victory, but it rings hollow. Technically the Chens were not entrapped but these violations could have been easily prevented with a simple 'No' [by the bribed officer]. This total exercise leads any critical observer to be skeptical and to ponder whether justice had been served."[12] Judge Tang's pondering in *Chen* inclined him to see the wisdom of Judge Peckham's judgment.

Bob Boochever had gone from New York to Alaska to pursue a career as a lawyer; he had eventually been elected chief justice of the Alaska Supreme Court by his fellow judges.[13] At the age of 63 in 1980, he had come to our court. He agreed with Judge Tang. The views of all three judges—Peckham, Tang, and Boochever—weighed heavily with me.

To these views were added that of the bench memo. In advance of the argument, Judge Tang, as presiding judge, had assigned the case to me, and I, in turn, had assigned it to one of my law clerks, Karl Tilleman, to prepare the bench memo. The bench memo—a summary of the facts, the decision of the district court, and the legal precedents—is the first look the appeals court takes at a case on appeal. In our court, contrary to the more general practice, the bench memo goes to all three members of the panel, serving them as a kind of aide-memoire and assuring each of them that they are seeing the same thing. It does not preempt the views of individual judges but does furnish a common starting point. In theory it is neutral; in practice, a law clerk almost always adopts his or her view of what the outcome should be. In this case, Karl, an outstanding graduate of Brigham Young University Law School, wrote a fifteen page memo (my idea of maximum length), meticulously setting out the arguments pro and con, quoting Judge Tang in *Chen* (a thoughtful

11. Thomas Tang (1922–95) was a Ninth Circuit judge from 1977 to 1993.

12. *United States v. Hsieh Hui Mei Chen*, 754 F.2d 817, 826 (9th Cir. 1985) (Tang, Cir. J., concurring).

13. Robert Boochever (1917–2011) served on the Alaska Supreme Court (1972–80; chief justice, 1975–78) and on the Ninth Circuit (1980–2011). The Alaska Constitution, Art. IV, § 2(b), provides that the chief justice of the state supreme court is selected from among themselves by the court's members for a three-year term.

touch) and concluding that Judge Peckham's "slight variance from the authorized guideline range cannot be deemed unreasonable."

Referring to the views of the others involved does not, of course, explain my vote. These influenced me. I had to decide for myself. What I put in the opinion for the court were the reasons for my decision. Judge Peckham made no mistake in finding on the facts before him that the defendants had not sought to make money out of the bribe to the agent and in finding that the agent had influenced them not to withdraw. Nothing showed that either defendant was in touch with the smugglers of human beings who might trade in green cards. Nothing in their backgrounds showed any other deviance from conventional conduct. Their acts were fairly characterized as aberrant. The Sentencing Commission itself, in 1991, declared in so many words that it had "not dealt with the single acts of aberrant behavior that still may justify probation at higher levels through departures."[14]

Read this way as "single acts of aberrant behavior," Akiko and Takai's conduct was clearly beyond the control of the Sentencing Guidelines. But could we fairly describe what they had done as "single acts?" Akiko and Takai had met and talked about the calls they made to the agent. They had made several calls. They had collected the bribe money. Takai had sent the plane ticket. Akiko had delivered the bribe. By an ordinary way of counting, there were seven to ten acts that they had performed, seven to ten times they had engaged in aberrant actions.

What occurred to me by way of analogy was the dispute over the morality of kidney transplants. It is generally agreed to be wrong to cut into a person's body and to cut out an organ; consent cannot morally be given to self-mutilation. But if the kidney is given to save the life of another person, the entire operation is moral. What are, singly, immoral actions are looked at as a whole, one moral act. So here, what were multiple actions formed a single criminal act. In the opinion I even addressed the existence of two crimes—the conspiracy and the delivery of the money. They were, I wrote, "so closely related that, for the purposes of deciding whether they are aberrant, they constitute a single act." I upheld Judge Peckham's sentence.

---

14. *Sentencing Guidelines Manual*, Ch. 1, Part A, Introduction, para. 4(d).

FIVE

# Her Voice, Herself[1]

FORD MOTOR COMPANY AND ITS ADVERTISING AGENCY, Young & Rubicam, Inc., in 1985 advertised the Ford Lincoln Mercury Sable with a series of nineteen 30 or 60 second television spots in what the agency called "The Yuppie Campaign." The aim was to make an emotional connection with Yuppies, bringing back memories of when they were in college. Different popular songs of the seventies were sung on each commercial. The agency tried to get "the original people," that is, the singers who had popularized the songs, to sing them. Failing in that endeavor in ten cases, the agency had the songs sung by "sound alikes."

One of the original people was Bette Midler. Her name was not familiar to me. I had no interest in her style of singing, nor had I ever seen any of her movies. I was even unsure about the pronunciation of her first name. Was it Betty as in Bette Davis or Bet as the French might say? My law clerks assured me that it was Bet. In a wider world than mine, she was nationally known as an actress and singer. She won a Grammy as early as 1973 as the Best New Artist of that year. Records made by her went Gold and Platinum. She was nominated in 1979 for an Academy award for Best Female Actress in *The Rose*, in which she portrayed a pop singer. Newsweek in its June 30, 1986 issue described her as an "outrageously original singer/comedian." Time spoke of her in its March 2, 1987 issue as "a legend" and "the most dynamic and poignant singer-actress of her time."

---

1. *Midler v. Ford Motor Co.*, 849 F.2d 460 (9th Cir. 1988), *appeal after remand*, 944 F.2d 909 (9th Cir. 1991).

When Young & Rubicam was preparing the Yuppie Campaign it presented one commercial to its client by playing an edited version of Midler singing "Do You Want To Dance?" taken from the 1973 Midler album, "The Divine Miss M." After the client accepted the idea and form of the commercial, the agency contacted Midler's manager, Jerry Edelstein. The conversation went as follows: "Hello, I am Craig Hazen from Young and Rubicam. I am calling you to find out if Bette Midler would be interested in doing...?" Edelstein: "Is it a commercial?" "Yes." "We are not interested."

Undeterred, Young & Rubicam sought out Uta Hedwig whom it knew to have been one of "the Harlettes," backup singers for Midler for ten years. Hedwig was told by Young & Rubicam that "they wanted someone who could sound like Bette Midler's recording of 'Do You Want To Dance?'" She was asked to make a "demo" tape of the song if she was interested . She made an a capella demo and got the job.

At the direction of Young & Rubicam, Hedwig then made a record for the commercial. The Midler record of "Do You Want To Dance?" was first played to her. She was told to leave out only a few "aahs" unsuitable for the commercial. Hedwig imitated Midler to the best of her ability.

After the commercial was aired, Midler was told by "a number of people" that it "sounded exactly" like her record of "Do You Want To Dance." Hedwig was told by "many personal friends" that they thought it was Midler singing the commercial. Ken Fritz, a personal manager in the entertainment business not associated with Midler, declared by affidavit that he heard the commercial on more than one occasion and thought Midler was doing the singing.

Midler brought suit in 1986 against both Ford and its agency. "The conduct of the average thief," the court called the defendants' behavior. "If we can't buy it, we'll take it." These unusually sharp words came from Ferdinand F. Fernandez, the shy and scholarly judge presiding over the case.[2] Like Tang, the son of an immigrant, in this case from Galicia, Fernandez had practiced law in Pomona, had served for five years as a superior court judge in San Bernardino County, and had been appointed to the district court for the central district of California in 1985. He was

2. Ferdinand F. Fernandez (born 1937) was a California superior court judge (1980–85) and a federal district judge (1985–89) before his appointment to the Ninth Circuit in 1989.

later to be my colleague on the circuit where I came to appreciate his conscientiousness and modesty.

Despite his denunciation of their behavior, Judge Fernandez granted summary judgment to the defendants. Midler, he ruled, had no viable claim for unfair competition, invasion of her privacy, or invasion of her right of publicity. The law of theft did not apply to imitation of a voice. Midler was seeking a remedy for a wrong that no case decided by a court of the state of California had ever recognized.

Her appeal was heard by a panel on which Judge Tang presided, I was a member, and the third judge was Procter Hug, Jr., 57-years-old, of Reno, Nevada, appointed to our court in 1977, whose sensibilities often coincided with mine.[3] I found in my colleagues a warm sympathy for the approach that I as the judge assigned to the case took. I thought from the start that Midler's case had problems but that a theft should not go unredressed.

Federal judges, hearing the case of a California plaintiff against entities incorporated outside California, we were sitting in diversity; that is, the plaintiff and the defendants were citizens of diverse states and as the amount in contention exceeded $10,000, Congress had provided a federal forum for the plaintiff's case. We were, however, applying the law of the state of California, not federal law. A famous opinion of Justice Brandeis, *Erie Railroad v. Tompkins*,[4] had directed federal courts sitting in diversity to apply the law of the state in which they sat. The opinion, still taught with enthusiasm when I went to law school, had left unresolved difficulties. Was one decision by an intermediate state court the law of the state for *Erie* purposes? Suppose the decisions of two intermediate state courts were in conflict as they often were in California? What was the force of dicta in a state court opinion? And, very much to the point in Midler's case, suppose a state court had never addressed the question. Did that mean that the plaintiff must lose because the tort she pointed to had never been recognized? Judge Fernandez had, with circumspection, so thought. Or could we boldly guess what the Supreme Court of California would say if asked the question and, guessing, declare that to be the decisive law?

3. Procter R. Hug, Jr. (1931–2019), served on the Ninth Circuit from 1977 to 2017 (chief judge 1996–2000).

4. 304 U.S. 64 (1938).

The First Amendment, of course, protected imitation of a voice when the purpose of the imitation was humorous or satirical. Just as one's face could be the subject of a cartoon, so one's voice could be mimicked in political ridicule. A voice as such was not sacred.

Federal copyright law occupied much of the area we were entering. Copyright protected "original works fixed in any tangible medium of expression." The copyright holder of "Do You Want To Dance?" had licensed Young & Rubicam to use the song. Midler could not claim a violation of copyright. Was not her suit an intrusion into space where copyright was decisive? Her voice was "fixed" in a "tangible medium." It was that fixed pattern of sound that Uta Hedwig had imitated. Her song was a copy of the record, and the copy had been made with permission of the owner of the copyright. This argument was seriously, even strenuously, maintained by the defendants. It would be the death of copyright if a copyright owner could not license singers as the owner chose.

Nancy Sinatra, in a case decided by the circuit in 1970, had failed to recover damages for an imitation of her recording of "These Boots Are Made For Walkin."[5] Young & Rubicam had made the recording for an advertising campaign on behalf of Goodyear Tire and Rubber Company. The song was closely identified with Nancy Sinatra, and the singers of the commercial imitated her voice and style and were said to have dressed and looked like her. The court held that the permission of the copyright holder, given to the company, was decisive. Copyright, being a matter of federal law, was preemptive. So here, Midler's claim, being at best a matter of state law, was said to fall before it.

The argument struck me as serious but not fatal. What the defendants had sought, and what they had obtained was more than an imitation of the copyrighted performance. They had obtained the impression for listeners that Bette Midler was singing for them. At least, if Midler's proof held up at trial, the defendants would be shown to have appropriated a part of her personality in order to provide a background for their ad. Her voice in the record was fixed in certain sounds. What the defendants had done was not to reproduce those exact sounds but the unfixed sounds of her voice in song. As for the Nancy Sinatra precedent, it was distinguishable. She had sued Goodyear Tire and Rubber for unfair competition. But she was not selling tires. She and the company were not competitors.

5. *Sinatra v. Goodyear Tire & Rubber Co.*, 435 F.2d 711 (9th Cir. 1970).

Midler's case was moulded differently. Unfair competition was not what she relied on.

A section of the Civil Code of California gave damages to a person injured by another who used the person's "name, voice, signature, photograph or likeness in any manner." That law didn't help Midler. The defendants hadn't used her voice. They hadn't mentioned her name. Had they used her likeness? Judge Fernandez, sensitive to language, had thought not. "Likeness" meant image, not sound-alike. But there was a germ of hope for her in this statute, which declared the remedies it provided were "cumulative" to those that existed at common law.[6] By implication, then, there might be a common law right and remedy.

A companion statute prohibited the use of a deceased person's name, voice, signature, photograph or likeness and described the rights it recognized as "property rights." By analogy the common law rights were property rights. Appropriation of such rights was a tort in California, so a case decided by the circuit in 1974 had held.[7] In a television commercial for Winston cigarettes the R.J. Reynolds Tobacco Company had used a photograph of a famous professional racing driver's racing car. The number of the car was changed and a wing-like device known as a "spoiler" was attached to the car; the car's features of white pinpointing, an oval medallion, and solid red coloring were retained. The driver, Lothar Motschenbacher, was in the car but his features were not visible. Some persons, viewing the commercial, correctly inferred that the car was his and that he was in the car and was therefore endorsing the product. The defendants were held to have invaded a "proprietary interest" of Motschenbacher in his own identity.

Midler's case was not quite the same as Motschenbacher's. He and his car were physically used by the tobacco company's ad; he made part of his living out of giving commercial endorsements. But as the circuit had expressed it in *Motschenbacher*, California recognized an injury from "an appropriation of the attributes of one's identity." As in *Motschenbacher*, the defendants here were using an imitation to convey the impression that Midler was singing for them.

---

6. Cal. Civ. Code § 3344. The "companion statute" in the next paragraph is § 3344.1(b).

7. *Motschenbacher v. R. J. Reynolds Tobacco Co.*, 498 F.2d 821 (9th Cir. 1974).

Why did the defendants ask Midler to sing, we asked ourselves, if her voice was not of value to them? Why did they studiously acquire the services of a sound-alike and instruct the Harlette to imitate Midler if Midler's voice was not of value to them? Was not its value what the market would have paid Midler to have sung the commercial in person?

A voice is more distinctive and more personal than the automobile accoutrements protected in *Motschenbacher.* A voice is as distinctive and personal as a face. The human voice is one of the most palpable ways identity is manifested. We are all aware that a friend is at once known by a few words on the phone. At a philosophical level it had been observed that with the sound of a voice, "the other stands before me."[8] A fortiori, these observations held true of singing. I thought in particular of my wife, Mary Lee, who, not a professional singer, loves to sing. The singer manifested herself in the song. To impersonate her voice was to steal her identity. Summary judgment for the defendants was reversed.

Our decision was not the end of the case. The defendants, as was their right, asked for "rehearing," a polite phrase meaning that the panel needed to rethink its decision. They also "suggested rehearing en banc," a phrase meaning "we want the whole court to take the case from this inept panel and reverse this crazy decision." Petitions for rehearing do not become so blunt in actual words but they often drop the deferential tone with which the lawyers have been addressing the court. Here, the defendants said simply that we had invented a new tort, with the result that "a wide array of ordinary advertising activities could become actionable, threatening commercial speech with little public benefit." We had been guilty, they added, of "judicial activism," creating a tort that Congress had declined to create. We read their cri de coeur and noted that we were expounding the common law of California, not a federal statute. No member of the panel changed his mind. No member of the court asked for an en banc. The mandate issued.

Still, the case was not over. All that had been established by our decision was that Midler was entitled to damages if she proved at trial the facts she had pointed to on her appeal. Reviewing summary judgment

8. *See* Don Idhe, *Listening and Voice: Phenomenologies of Sound* 77 (1976; 2d ed. 2007). Idhe (1924–2024) wrote extensively on the philosophy of technology, and *Listening and Voice* is widely seen as a groundbreaking study in the phenomenological investigation of sound.

for her opponent, we assumed these facts to be true. We had not found them to be true in fact. The case was returned to the district court.

By 1989, the date the case was actually tried, Judge Fernandez had been appointed to the circuit. His place was taken by A. Wallace Tashima, who had to apply the law of our decision.[9] Judge Tashima, like Judge Fernandez, was later to be my colleague on the circuit. The first person of Japanese ancestry to serve on our court, he was a tower of common sense and uncommon sensibility.

Uta Hedwig, the Harlette, turned out to be a stellar witness for Midler. She testified that she had been told to sound as much like Midler as possible. The law, as we had put it, was that the defendants were liable if they sought "to convey the impression that Midler was singing for them." Nonetheless, the defendants moved for a directed verdict claiming that there was no evidence that they had attempted to imitate Midler's voice, only the copyrighted singing of the song. Judge Tashima denied the motion and then admirably instructed the jury on what was not before it:

> Most of you are familiar with the term "copyright." Copyright law protects authors of original works, such as the song "Do You Want to Dance?" There are no issues of copyright law, as such, for you to decide in this case. However, in deciding whether or not Young & Rubicam deliberately imitated Bette Midler's voice, you must keep in mind that Young & Rubicam had the right to use the song "Do You Want to Dance?" You must also keep in mind that the mere imitation of a performance contained in a recording is not a violation of the copyright law.

Knowing that it was the imitation of her voice on which they must focus, the jury returned a verdict for Midler, finding the value of what the defendants had deprived her of to be $400,000. Judge Tashima ruled that Midler could not get punitive damages. She could not show that Young & Rubicam had had an "evil motive," especially since "the tort in question has only recently been discovered"—a polite reference to the novelty of our initial decision.

Again, we heard the appeal, it being customary for the panel that has decided one appeal to reserve the right to hear the second if it so chooses. There was little to argue. A memorandum disposition affirming Judge

---

9. A. Wallace Tashima (born 1934) served as a district judge (1980–96) before his appointment to the Ninth Circuit in 1996.

Tashima—a memdispo as I style this sort of judicial action—did the job. It was efficiently written by my law clerk, Julie Knox, and not published. The defendants, being fully solvent, had no choice but to pay.

I had one further concern. Our decision on the first appeal had established the tort of taking a professional singer's voice for the profit of the takers. We were only a federal court stating what we thought a California state court would hold. The California state courts could say that we were mistaken, that no such tort existed in the state. As of this writing, *Midler v. Ford Motor Company* has not been repudiated by California.[10]

10. This remains true as of August 2025.

SIX

# The Hillsborough Physician[1]

AT 8:00 P.M. ON THE EVENING OF JUNE 25, 1983, Dr. James Hutchinson, a resident of Hillsborough for twenty years, was strolling near his home. He was hailed from a police cruiser by Officer John Grant, a Hillsborough policeman, who asked Dr. Hutchinson to identify himself. Dr. Hutchinson replied that he was Dr. Hutchinson. He added that he was a resident of Hillsborough. Officer Grant swung his car around, got out, and, leaving a police dog in the cruiser, approached Dr. Hutchinson and asked him to stop. Dr. Hutchinson continued walking. Officer Grant took hold of him, took away his walking cane, marched him to the patrol car, patted him down, and handcuffed him. Shortly thereafter, Officer Ransom arrived and identified Dr. Hutchinson as a resident of the community, and he was released.

These facts were undisputed by Dr. Hutchinson and Officer Grant. When Dr. Hutchinson sued Officer Grant and the Town of Hillsborough for violation of his civil rights, the federal district judge, John Vukasin,[2] could see little in dispute between the parties. On these facts, he gave summary judgment to the defendants.

Other facts, however, were in dispute. The disputes were three:

---

1. *Hutchinson v. Grant*, 796 F.2d 288 (9th Cir. 1986). This Hillsborough is in California.

2. John P. Vukasin, Jr. (1928–93), was a California superior court judge (1974–83) before his service on the federal district court (1983–93).

1. How Dr. Hutchinson responded to Officer Grant. Dr. Hutchinson said that he extended his hand in greeting. Officer Grant said that Dr. Hutchinson's behavior was uncooperative and evasive.
2. What Officer Grant said to Dr. Hutchinson after he first addressed him. Dr. Hutchinson said that Officer Grant said, "I don't give a damn about nigger walkers." Officer Grant denied saying anything of the sort.
3. The force with which Dr. Hutchinson was handcuffed. Dr. Hutchinson said that he was wrenched and that he was forced over the hood of the patrol car. Officer Grant acknowledged only that he had handcuffed him.

These disputes made *Hutchinson v. Grant* a classic instance of a district judge jumping the gun and resolving issues that should have been left to the jury to decide. Everything turned on who the jury believed, or so it seemed before the defendants' excuse was considered.

The defendants' excuse rested on a confusion of names and identities. In May 1983, the Hillsborough police had arrested a man who called himself Captain Peter Hutchinson. He was convicted of trespassing and vandalism and put on probation for a year. He was released from custody just eleven days before the incident with Dr. Hutchinson. Shortly after his release, there was a break-in at the same vacant house where Peter Hutchinson had trespassed in May. The police guessed that he had returned to the scene of his earlier crimes. They began to patrol the areas regularly, looking for Peter Hutchinson. When James Hutchinson identified himself as a doctor, it seemed like a variant on Peter's title of captain.

The law was and is clear. A policeman cannot arrest you without having a warrant for you or, alternatively, having probable cause that you have just committed a crime or are committing a crime or are about to commit a crime. The wonderful clarity of this rule, and the wonderful protection it affords all of us from harassment by overzealous officers, were lessened by the Supreme Court in *Terry v. Ohio*.[3] The court held that the brief detention of "a suspicious individual" in order to obtain more information before releasing him was permissible police practice. If the police officer feared for his own safety, he might use force in effecting this "momentary" stop.

---

3. 392 U.S. 1 (1968).

The so-called *Terry* stop was a category into which Officer Grant might fit what he had done. He had reason to be suspicious of a Hutchinson. He might well consider one so recently convicted of a crime would use force against him. He released the doctor once he knew his true identity. As a *Terry*-stopper, he was immune.

So the case looked on appeal, arguably not certain as to how it should come out. My colleagues were Harry Pregerson, the bravest of judges in defending the rights of any disadvantaged person, and Cecil F. Poole, formerly a district judge and before that, United States Attorney in San Francisco, of historic significance as the first African American on our court.[4] Assigned the case by Judge Pregerson, I was conscious that both colleagues resonated to the plaintiff's complaint.

One or two facts were not in the record but in my mind. First, the nature of Hillsborough. Situated on the peninsula south of San Francisco, it was an enclave of luxury, in which the number of African American homeowners might be counted on one hand. Second, pedestrians there were probably rare, if I could judge from San Marino, California, a comparable haven that I knew better. Walking itself was suspicious to some citizens of such a place. Thirdly, it was eminently understandable why a physician, who had earned the income to live in Hillsborough, who had lived there for twenty years, and who was engaged in a post-prandial excursion should feel outraged when he was accosted, halted, deprived of his walking stick, handcuffed, bent over a police car and referred to with a racial epithet.

The racial slur may have spurred his suit, but I could imagine how I would have felt taking a walk after dinner in Berkeley (where only a few warm nights would ever encourage an excursion) and being set upon by an ungracious patrolman. The legal test was whether Officer Grant had objective reasons for making the stop. Whether he did or not depended on the jury's ascertainment of all the facts. What was evident to me by way of empathy was that Dr. Hutchinson had suffered an outrage which he was entitled to have tried.

We agreed that the Town of Hillsborough had not been shown to be liable. We reversed the district court and remanded for trial as to Officer Grant. Undoubtedly, his insurance company was the ultimate defendant.

---

4. See above, pages 13 n.2 & 16 n.7.

Officer Grant did not seek rehearing. Five months after our decision, the case was settled.

I did not know of the settlement nor did I have any inkling of what had happened after we had acted until a decade later. Then Mary Lee and I received an invitation to dinner on the Peninsula. The hostess we barely knew as a friend of friends. She told us that she was a friend of Dr. Hutchinson, that he would like to meet me, and that she was inviting him and his wife. From that information I gleaned that Dr. Hutchinson must have been satisfied by the outcome of the litigation. I looked forward to meeting him.

The meeting was not a disappointment. He was a graceful man with a gracious manner. His wife was charming. They told us of their daughter who had studied music in Paris. We did not mention the case. For the first, and so far the only time, I saw a figure who was a name in one of my opinions turn into a person of flesh and blood. There was unusual pleasure in the experience.

SEVEN

# The Mocababoo[1]

THE CALIFORNIA AND HAWAII SUGAR COMPANY—C & H, to use its common abbreviation—needed a vessel of vast proportions to transport its annual sugar crop from Hawaii to its refinery in Crockett, California. In its wisdom, C & H in 1979 decided to construct two vehicles—a barge to carry the sugar and a tug to push the barge. C & H hired two companies to do the job. Halter Marine, a Louisiana corporation, would construct the tug and deliver it for connection. Sun Ship, a Pennsylvania company, would make the barge and connect the tug. In Hawaiian, the barge and the integrated vessel were described as a Mocababoo or push boat.

Neither barge nor tug was cheap. C & H agreed to pay $25,400,000 for the barge and $20,350,000 for the tug. In drafting the contracts, each party was represented by a team of negotiators and by counsel. C & H expressed particular concern that the Mocababoo be ready by June 30, 1981. The vessel was to replace the shipping that the Matson line had previously provided. Sugar is seasonal, with seventy percent of the harvest occurring between April and October. Roughly one million tons a year were grown in Hawaii. Storage on the islands accommodated only a quarter of the crop. The vision of "a mountain of sugar piling up in Hawaii" was in front of the negotiators as they thought about what the damages should be if either shipbuilder did not meet the June deadline.

1. *California & Hawaiian Sugar Co. v. Sun Ship, Inc.*, 794 F.2d 1433, 1434 (9th Cir. 1986), *amended*, 811 F.2d 1264 (9th Cir. 1987).

In separate contracts, it was agreed that, in default, Halter should pay $10,000 per day and that Sun Ship should pay $17,000 per day.

What seems to have been beyond the imagination of these experienced negotiators was that both Halter and Sun Ship would default. Who, if anyone, would be liable then? But that is what happened. Sun Ship completed the barge in March 1982. Halter completed the tug in July of the same year. The Mocababoo was over a year late in arriving in Hawaii.

C & H did not let the sugar rot. It found other shipping. It also invoked the terms of its contracts with the shipbuilders. Halter settled, for what amount we were not told. Sun Ship paid C & H $ 17,000 a day from June 30, 1981 to January 1982, then thought better of it, and denied liability. What harm had Sun Ship done C & H when the tug was lacking? C & H answered this question with a lawsuit in the federal district court for Northern California. Judge Vukasin gave judgment to C & H. Sun Ship appealed.

Our panel was composed of ex-academics, not a frequent occurrence. Presiding was Dorothy W. Nelson, who had come to the court from the deanship of the law school of the University of Southern California, a person of wide sympathies and quick perception.[2] Joining her was Bill Canby, once a Supreme Court law clerk, once a Peace Corps director in Africa, and more recently a professor of law at Arizona State and an authority on American Indian law, a cosmopolitan and careful judge.[3] I had just come from Boalt. I was particularly pleased to be assigned a case that involved no new area of law but was embedded in the Anglo-American law of contract.

Two questions were presented to us, neither one of which seemed to me to have obvious answers. The first was the question pressed by Sun Ship. What possible difference had its default made to C & H? If it had performed on time, C & H would have had a useless barge on its hands, a liability, not an asset. Sun Ship's point merged with the second question. Were the damages of $17,000 per day a penalty that the law should

2. Dorothy Wright Nelson (born 1928) was appointed to the Ninth Circuit in 1979. Before her appointment, she was on the faculty of the Southern California Gould School of Law (from 1957 on, dean 1968–80).

3. William C. Canby, Jr. (born 1931) was appointed to the Ninth Circuit in 1980. He was a clerk to Justice Charles E. Whittaker (1958–59), and a member of the Arizona State University law faculty (1967–80).

not enforce? If C & H had suffered no setback, what else could the monetary amounts be but a penalty? *The Merchant of Venice* swam into my mind. In exacting the bond, did not C & H in Shylock's phrase "crave the law" and did it not deserve to be thwarted by an equitable reading of the law like Portia's?[4]

Were my sympathies in a subterranean way engaged in a different direction? C & H was an agricultural cooperative formed by fourteen sugar plantations in Hawaii. Its name united my state to its attractive Pacific neighbor. Its plant at Crockett was a familiar sight on any trip to the wine country. That out-of-state corporations will be "home-teamed" when they are sued is a familiar fear, leading them to prefer the federal forum to state judges. I was not conscious of any preference for C & H except that I like sugar, especially sugar as it played a part in desserts, cookies, and candy.

The sugar involved in our case, I learned, was crushed cane in the shape of coarse brown crystal. Only at Crockett would it be transformed into the white stuff to be sold to groceries for home consumption and to the soft drink, candy, and cereal companies that were its intermediate consumers. My fondness for chocolate did not translate into a bias for C & H. My two colleagues were equally without detectable feelings in favor of either litigant. Each of the parties was represented by large, old-line San Francisco firms who spiritedly directed our attention to what should be the law.

That law had to be Pennsylvania's. The contract so prescribed. We were sitting in diversity. Federal precedents were not apt. That meant we should start with Pennsylvania's version of the Uniform Commercial Code, a statute drawn up by a multi-state commission to provide certainty in common commercial situations. Certainty on our subject, however, was dissolved by the statute. Liquidated damages—that is, damages expressed in dollars—the statute said were to be considered reasonable and therefore enforceable "in the light of anticipated or actual harm." Anticipated or actual—that was our question. Did we look at the anticipated or the actual harm to C & H?

The U.C.C.'s alternative possibilities mirrored the approach of the *Restatement (Second) of Contracts*. In this text the law was set out by no

4. Act IV scene 1 line 212. The manuscript reads "Portia's phrase," obviously a typographical error.

legislature. The law was declared by a committee of lawyers, law professors, and judges organized by the American Law Institute, a self-perpetuating collection of professionals who had been at work since 1920[5] rationalizing areas of law and presenting the results of their deliberations in concise, citable form. Armed with no greater authority than the prestige of their members and the wisdom of their conclusions, the various Restatements occupied a place in the legal firmament that sometimes sparkled more brightly than any statute or case. Pure positivists, who believe that law only issues from duly-constituted legal authorities, were refuted daily by the way the Restatements functioned.

Like the U.C.C. commissioners, the authors of the *Restatement of Contracts* aimed for certainty. After offering the alternatives of actual or anticipated loss, the Restatement went on in Comment (b) to tip in one direction: "the amount fixed is reasonable to the extent that it approximates the loss anticipated at the time of the making of the contract, even though it may not approximate the actual loss."[6] That appeared to plump for reasonable anticipated loss. But what the Restatement stated did not have to be taken as the last word.

I started with the ambiguous statute, moved on to the less ambiguous Restatement, but returned to the common law of Pennsylvania. The common law of Pennsylvania was, more or less, Anglo-American common law as molded by the courts of the state. There were strong indications that the U.C.C. should be read in light of the common law. Prior to the adoption of the U.C.C., Pennsylvania had enforced liquidated damage clauses that its courts labeled as nonpenal, but equitable considerations relating to the actual harm incurred were taken into account along with the difficulty of proving damages if a liquidated damage clause was rejected. In a single lower court case, decided after the U.C.C.'s enactment, a Pennsylvania court had stated that if liquidated damages appear unreasonable in light of the harm suffered, "the contractual provision will be voided as a penalty."[7]

That case, however, was not on all fours with our case: It had involved a contract between parties of unequal bargaining power; the contract was characterized by the court as "a clever attempt to secure both the

5. The ALI was formally established in 1923.

6. Restatement (Second) of Contracts § 356 cmt. (b) (1981).

7. *Unit Vending Corp. v. Tobin Enterprises*, 168 A.2d 750, 751 (Pa. Super. 1961).

penny and the cake" by the party with superior strength. In the jargon of the profession, it was "an adhesion contract," the kind in which the customer takes the terms printed on the sales slip of the ticket seller or parking garage. An adhesion contract is looked at with suspicion by a court. Mechanically to read this Pennsylvania case as the law governing our case would have been a mistake. It did constitute an attempt to interpret the governing statute humanely and equitably.

I returned to the *Restatement*, Comment (b), the very comment that had seemed so helpful and to favor the use of anticipated damages. Comment (b) had gone on to say that if the difficulty of proof of loss is slight, then actual damages might be the measure of unreasonableness: "If, to take an extreme case, it is clear that no loss at all has occurred, a provision fixing a substantial sum as damages is unenforceable. See Illustration 4." Illustration 4 was a case of a contractor, A, agreeing to build B's race track by a specific date and to pay B $1,000 a day for every day's delay. A delayed a month, but B did not get permission to operate the track during that month, so B suffered no loss. The *Restatement* characterized the $1,000 per day as an unenforceable penalty. Sun contended that it was in the position of A. No actual loss had been suffered by C & H because C & H had no tug to mate with the barge.

But the *Restatement* dealt with a case where the defaulting contractor was alone in his default. We faced a case of concurrent defaults. If we were to be so literal-minded as to follow the Restatement here, we would have to conclude that because both parties were in default, C & H suffered no damage until one party performed. Not until the barge was ready in March 1982 could C & H hold Halter for damages, and then only for the period after that date. The continued default of both parties would operate to take each of them off the hook for most of their defaults. That conclusion seemed to me a *reductio ad absurdum*. Doubling the default would let both defaulters go unscathed. "That cannot be the law," I concluded.

What came into my mind was an old tort problem: A pushes C out of a window. B shoots C as he falls. Who is liable for C's death? Both A and B, because they are each a substantial cause of the injury. So Sun Ship and Halter were substantial causes of C & H's injury. Both should be held liable.

Once I was convinced that the absence of the tug could not absolve Sun Ship, I turned to the reasonableness of the damages that the contract had provided. A troubling fact was that the cost of Halter's default had been calculated at only $10,000 a day, Sun Ship's at $17,000. Didn't the discrepancy demonstrate that Sun Ship was being asked to pay a penalty? My opinion ducked the question, which I resolved mentally by noting that Sun Ship was getting over five million dollars more than Halter and so might be persuaded to promise a larger sum as compensation for its failure to perform.[8] The question remained for me, Was $17,000 a reasonable measure of the harm C & H could foresee at the time the contract was formed? Or, to put the same question another way, wasn't what it had actually cost to get more shipping in 1981 pretty close to what could have been anticipated in 1979? The actual damages C & H had suffered, after subtracting what it would have cost to have operated the Mocababoo, were only $368,000. Didn't that figure prove that the anticipated damages were unreasonable?

C & H answered these questions with a Pennsylvania decision—one fairly recently decided (1971) and made by the Pennsylvania Supreme Court. A contractor had failed to perform a municipal contract. The actual loss to the borough was $1,000. The contract provided that he pay $45,000 on default. He was made to pay $45,000. The Pennsylvania Supreme Court approved.[9]

The case, however, was far from decisive. It did not apply the Uniform Commercial Code. Rules appropriate for bids to governments were sufficiently different from those applicable between private parties to prevent our automatic adoption of this precedent. I continued to look for guidance.

The Law and Economics people, it occurred to me, must have given attention to this sector of the law where precise sums of money played such a part. With delight I turned up an opinion by Judge Richard Posner, the most brilliant of academics on the federal bench. Judge Posner reported litigation had blurred the line between a proper and a penal clause. The distinction between them, Judge Posner had written, is "not an easy one to draw in practice."[10] But practice was where I was, and I had to draw the line.

8. The manuscript reads "getting more than five million dollars than Halter."
9. *Bellefonte Borough Auth. v. Gateway Equip. & Supply Co.*, 277 A.2d 347 (Pa. 1971).
10. *Lake River Corp. v. Carborundum Co.*, 769 F.2d 1284, 1290 (7th Cir. 1985).

I went back to Pennsylvania, this time over 150 years to the words of a venerated chief justice of the state, John Gibson. "Where each of the parties is content to take the risk of its turning out in a particular way," Chief Justice Gibson had written, "why should one be released from the contract, if there were no misrepresentation or other want of fair dealing?"[11] This rhetorical question resonated with me as stating a proposition situated at the heart of contract law. If one party did not have the other at a disadvantage, if both parties were represented by counsel, if it was not an adhesion contract, why should the court rewrite it? The parties negotiating in 1979 were in a position to estimate the risks that would be run and the damages that might ensue if the Mocababoo were not delivered on time. Who were we to retroactively second guess them?

Although it was not necessary, I took further comfort from an exposition of the common law of contracts by the House of Lords in 1905.[12] The defendant shipyard had agreed to pay 500 pounds per week per vessel for delay in the delivery of four torpedo boat destroyers to the Spanish Navy in 1897. The shipyard pointed out that had the destroyers been delivered on schedule they would have been sunk with the rest of the Spanish Navy by the Americans in 1898. The House of Lords found the defense unpersuasive. To prove damages the whole administration of the Spanish Navy would have had to have been investigated. The House of Lords refused to undertake such a difficult investigation when the parties had made an honest effort in advance to set in monetary terms what the lack of the destroyers would mean to Spain.

This decision in favor of foreign plaintiffs suing a firm of importance to the British navy struck one as the triumph, the apotheosis even, of sound contract law. In those days I did my own research. I discovered the case, *Clydebank Engineering & Shipbuilding Co. v. Yzquierdo y Castaneda*, among the English Reports in our court library. Uncited by the litigants, it could have been left unmentioned by me. But I could not refrain from remembrance of this glorious affirmation of principle.

---

11. *Ashcom v. Smith*, 2 Pen. & W. 211, 218–19 (Pa. 1830). John Banister Gibson (1780–1853) was a formidable judicial figure in antebellum American law. He served as a trial judge before being appointed to the Pennsylvania Supreme Court (1816–53, chief justice 1838–51). His successor as chief justice, Jeremiah S. Black, described Gibson as "the greatest mind" he had ever encountered.

12. *Clydebank Engineering & Shipbuilding Co. v. Yzquierdo y Castaneda*, 1905 A.C. 6.

After all the back and forth that I experienced in writing the opinion, after all the consultation of statutes and cases and commentaries, after all the signs pointing this way and that, I felt that our decision rested on a firm foundation. Promises are to be kept. The principle not only gives life to human society. Promise-making is one human activity that other animals cannot engage in.

Sun Ship, noting the zigzag course my opinion took, did not believe its foundation was so firm. The company filed for rehearing and for rehearing en banc. Rehearing en banc was highly unlikely. Why would the full court want to review a case determining the contract law of the state of Pennsylvania?

The panel was a different matter. Neither of my colleagues had had the experience of working through all the turns and twists that writing the opinion took. Each of them was curious and alert and open to persuasion and possessed of law clerks who would review Sun Ship's petition and might stir their doubts. It had taken me two months to write the opinion and have them agree to it. It took over eight months to resolve the questions raised by Sun Ship's petition. Portia's ghost hovered over us. In the end, Judge Nelson quietly indicated that she would have granted the petition. Judge Canby stayed with me.

The case had one consequence in legal education, of which I was unaware until I began to write this chapter. Checking the spelling of Mocababoo on Google, my secretary, Evelyn Lew, found a single entry. It was an examination question given at Boalt Hall to a class in contracts. Unlike many exam questions, this question was no hypothetical. It reproduced exactly the facts and issues of our case with the names of the parties and of the vessel unchanged. Forty-five minutes were allowed to answer the question, "What are the rights and duties of C & H and Sun?" A student could allot more time to answer if needed.

The professor giving the exam was an old colleague and friend, Melvin Eisenberg. He was also the Reporter for one of the American Law Institute's celebrated Restatements.[13] Finding the case reset by him in this context, posed by this professor, I thought that I had not exaggerated its difficulty.

---

13. Professor Eisenberg (born 1934) was the chief reporter for the Institute's *Principles of Corporate Governance: Analysis and Recommendations* (1992) and an adviser on three Restatements.

EIGHT

# The Sacramental Confession, Taped[1]

NO INSTITUTION WAS MORE INGRAINED in the Catholicism of my youth than the practice by which a priest, acting in the name of God, pardoned a person who had just confessed his or her sins. In Catholic thought it was God, not the priest, who pardoned, and it was God, not the priest, to whom one confessed. Through audible signs inaudible and invisible grace was conferred by the priest's act of absolution.

The sacrament was commonly called the Sacrament of Penance, because a penance—usually the saying of a certain number of Our Fathers and/or Hail Marys—was prescribed by the priest. Today, the practice is more often called the Sacrament of Reconciliation. Yesterday or today, the heart of the practice was the act of confession, the articulation to another person of sins committed since the last confession. The sins would include not only actions with physical effects but thoughts or merely movements of the mind to which consent had been given. Confession included what only the confessant could know.

The role of the priest hearing confession was compared at times to that of a judge, at times to that of a doctor. Like a judge he had to determine the gravity of the offense in order to set the penance. Like a doctor he was supposed to heal the wounded soul, using the medicines of encouragement and hope as well as of forgiveness. Sometimes the secular analogy was advanced of the psychoanalyst in psychoanalysis. None of the quotidian analogies communicated the sense that in confession there was oral interchange with the divine.

---

1. *Mockaitis v. Harcleroad*, 104 F.3d 1522 (9th Cir. 1997).

Against this background you may imagine my surprise when I was presented with an appeal centered on the taping of a confession, a taping that the prosecutor planned to introduce in a prosecution for murder. Was I so appalled at the intrusion that I was not an appropriate person to judge its lawfulness? The question is not free from difficulty.

The American system of selecting judges produces not a professional corps of jurists but persons representative of broad sections of public sectors distinguished by race, ethnicity, and religion. The belief is built into the system that fairness results from this mix of basic backgrounds. For an African-American judge to recuse himself in a case where justice to a black man was at issue would mean less fairness than if the judge participated. Analogously, I think that, in a country divided between believers and secularists, for a judge with religious beliefs to disqualify himself in a case where those beliefs frame the issue may subtract a sensitivity to the subject that promotes fairness. Should a Sabbatarian disqualify himself in a case where the issue is the constitutionality of a holiday on Saturday for Sabbatarians? In the case at hand, the parties did not ask me to recuse myself. My colleagues did not question my impartiality. And I did not raise the question that I now retroactively, and with some difficulty, answer.[2]

---

2. In *Feminist Women's Health Ctr. v. Codispoti*, 69 F.3d 399 (9th Cir. 1995), Judge Noonan denied a motion that he recuse himself because of his Roman Catholic beliefs from sitting on a case involving abortion. He later reflected at length on the fundamental issues raised by the motion and his decision. *See* John T. Noonan, Jr., *The Religion of the Justice: Does It Affect Constitutional Decision Making?*, 42 Tulsa L. Rev. 761, 765–66 (2007):

> To my mind, the decisive precedent was offered by Thurgood Marshall. Before being a judge, Marshall had been very active in the cause of racial justice, in particular as counsel for the NAACP. Marshall on that account did not recuse himself in cases where justice to African Americans was an issue. It would have been absurd for him to do so. He had been appointed because he understood these issues. I concluded that an American judge was not expected to come to a court without commitments on the great public issues of his day and that on abortion, in particular, neither a pro-abortion or anti-abortion history constituted disqualifying bias if one could judge the case before one fairly. The appearance of bias that one's history suggested could not be a factor if American judges were to come, as they did come, out of a highly political process. I added, for good measure, that Orthodox Judaism, the Mormon Church, and many Protestant denominations viewed abortion as sinful. Were only approvers of abortion fit to judge the case of an

The case began with the arrest of Jonathan Wayne Susbauer and Conan Wayne Hale for burglary and murder. Susbauer admitted to the police of Eugene, Oregon, that he and Hale had committed two burglaries in Eugene, one on December 14 and another on December 19, 1995. Susbauer also admitted to two detectives from the Lane County sheriff's office that he and Hale had participated in the killing on December 20 of three young persons, Kristal Bendele, Patrick Finley, and Brandon Williams. According to Susbauer, Hale and he had taken turns shooting them with a single .38 caliber pistol.

Hale's story was different. He told a county detective that he had been at a logging landing in a remote area near McGowen Creek with the

---

abortion provider? I did not think that judicial impartiality required so much. If every judge who was pro- or anti-abortion were disqualified from deciding an abortion case, the judiciary would be crippled. The same holds true as to every great issue on which public opinion is divided and on which every politically conscious person has convictions, often formed or aided by his religious commitments. To make those commitments a test for holding judicial office would violate, or come dangerously close to violating, Article VI of the Constitution and its ban on religious tests.

What enters into a judge's judgment is the judge's experience of life. It is not the party of the president who appointed him, a peculiarly gross way of predicting or accounting for the judge's acts, although a way often mechanically adopted by journalists. It is not solely the judge's prior experience as a litigator, a prosecutor, a bureaucrat, a corporate counselor, a civil rights activist, or a law teacher, although any one of such careers will have contributed to the judge's thinking. It is not solely the judge's childhood or his relations with his parents or his relationship to his spouse or to his children, if he has any. All of these relationships help mold the mind, the sensibility, the capacity for empathy that affect judgment. Education at every level from kindergarten to law school makes a difference too, in the best way by enabling the judge to make distinctions, see implications, and comprehend complexities and depth. In short, myriad are the influences that have gone into making the judge the person the judge is. The small segment of experience constituted by religious belief must mesh with the rest of the myriad. It was once written in praise of Henry James that he "had too fine a mind to have an idea," that is, James could not be read as writing from anything but an empathetic identification with the characters he cherished as persons. So, too, a judge should be seen as responding to the persons in the case before him, bringing not ideology but the response of a person to a person within the context cast by law. That response should be shaped by conscience.

three victims when they were killed. He said that he had struck Finley and Williams with a baseball bat. He denied killing them. Hale also admitted a part in the burglaries.

These admissions of the two suspects were recorded in affidavits of the officers to whom they had spoken. Certain details were corroborated. A witness had seen the three victims enter a truck where Hale was a passenger near the time of the murders. The pistol used in the murders matched the pistol stolen in the December 19 burglary. Sales of other property stolen in the burglaries had been traced to both suspects. The body of Patrick Finley was clothed in a rabbit fur jacket stolen in the December 19 burglary. The Eugene police and District Attorney F. Douglas Harcleroad had little doubt that they had the right men in custody.

Housed in the county jail since December 27, Hale asked a supervisor to arrange for a Catholic priest to visit him for the purpose of hearing his confession. On the morning of April 22, 1996, Father Timothy Mockaitis, a priest whose assignment included the jail, came to one of its visiting booths and, separated from Hale by glass, communicated with him by phone. The conversation was recorded, delivered to District Attorney Harcleroad's office by a sheriff's detective, James Carley, and sealed.

Harcleroad, rather curiously, then took steps to get judicial approval of a search warrant authorizing him to seize the tape already in his office. Carley signed an affidavit Harcleroad prepared setting out the taping and adding this theological information:

> I know from my experience and training that the Catholic confession is an integral part of Catholicism. It is a sacrament. The basic tenet of confession is that a person is absolved of his or her wrongdoing upon making a full and complete acknowledgment of what that wrongdoing is. After the person gives that acknowledgment of what he or she has done wrong, the priest prescribes a penance. Upon performance of the penance, a person is absolved of his or her sins.

The affidavit went on to its climax:

> Based on the aforesaid information, your affiant has probable cause to believe, and does believe, that evidence of the crime of murder, to wit: a statement by Conan Wayne Hale can be seized from an audio tape located in the office of the Lane County District Attorney, 125 East 8th Avenue, Eugene, Oregon.

Bryan Hodges, district court judge for Lane County, issued the requested warrant.[3] Carley executed it by turning over the tape to Harcleroad and unsealing it. Two deputy district attorneys listened to it. The tape was transcribed.

The existence of the tape did not remain a secret. It became a news item. On May 7, 1996, representatives of Francis E. George, archbishop of Portland, met with Harcleroad to request the tape's destruction and a guarantee of no further taping of sacramental confession in the jail. They were unsuccessful. On May 22, 1996, Harcleroad moved the county court to retain and seal the tape and to prohibit anyone who knew its contents from divulging them without further order of the court. Without a hearing or notice to anyone else, Judge Kip Leonard granted the order.[4]

On June 12, 1996, Father Mockaitis and Archbishop George filed a petition and motion in the county circuit court seeking the destruction of the tape and a continuation of the order as to the secrecy of the tape's contents. They asserted that the taping and its preservation violated both the federal and the state constitutions and federal and state statutes. They supported their claim with an affidavit as to the Sacrament of Penance in Catholic belief, filed by the Reverend Michael Maslowsky, a representative of Archbishop George, and by Father Mockaitis's own affidavit, in which he stated that as long as the tape remained in existence, "I feel uncomfortable in administering the Sacrament of Penance (Reconciliation) in the Lane County Jail."

The petition was routed to another judge of the county circuit, Jack A. Billings, to whom Hale's case had been assigned, Hale having been indicted on May 30 for aggravated murder.[5] Judge Billings immediately wrote counsel that the clerk did not know what to do with "this packet of papers" but that the attempt of "the clergy" to intervene in the criminal case was "not permitted by law." Judge Billings returned the packet together with the filing fee. Without hearing any party, he also entered this order:

3. Bryan T. Hodges (1940–2022) was an Oregon district and later circuit court judge from 1974 to 2006.

4. Kip W. Leonard (born 1948) was an Oregon district (1986–89) and then circuit (1989–2010) court judge.

5. Jack A. Billings (born 1946) was an Oregon circuit court judge (1993–2011).

> IT IS HEREBY ORDERED that all judicial officers and agents of the State who are now in possession or who may come into possession of a tape recording and transcript thereof of a conversation between Defendant and the Rev. Timothy Mockaitis which occurred on or about April 22, 1996 at the Lane Country Jail are to preserve those items as evidence in the above-styled cause during the pendency of these proceedings.

Thoroughly rebuffed by the county, the priest and his archbishop turned to the federal courts. They invoked their right to religious freedom under the First Amendment and their right to be free from unreasonable search under the Fourth Amendment, plus a variety of federal and state statutes. Their suit was opposed by Harcleroad and, surprisingly, by Hale himself. Hale went on to disclose the content of his confession:

> During my conversation with Father Mockaitis at the Lane County Jail on or about April 22, 1996, I made confession and asked for God to forgive me for the following transgressions: (1) for crimes of burglary which I committed with Jonathan Susbauer; (2) for being angry with and unable to forgive Susbauer for Susbauer having killed the three teenagers and for lying to the authorities about my involvement; and (3) for being angry with the District Attorney for believing Susbauer instead of me. I told Father Mockaitis that I did not commit any of the crimes people were accusing me of except the burglaries.

Hale's confession, in short, was very far from a confession of the murders. At most, it was a confession of burglaries he had already admitted. And it was a declaration of innocence as to the capital crimes, a declaration that Hale wanted to put forward "as evidence in my defense."

What use was the confession, then, to Harcleroad? So far as I could see, none. Yet he persisted in seeking to preserve the tape and to argue for its admissibility. What first appeared to be at stake for him was the value of the case as precedent for future tapings of confessions; but even that reason was disavowed in the federal district court. According to the district judge quoting the district attorney:

> Harcleroad himself admits that the taping was wrong: "There are some things which are legal and ethical but are simply not right. I have concluded that tape recording confidential clergy-penitent communications falls within the zone of societally unacceptable conduct."

The judge was Owen M. Panner, an Oklahoma lawyer who had moved to Oregon and in 1980 had been appointed to the district court.[6] An elder of the Presbyterian Church, he enjoyed a reputation for fairness. He agreed with Harcleroad that the taping had been wrong. Nonetheless, he declined to suppress the tape. Federal precedent, he thought, instructed a federal court not to interfere with an ongoing state prosecution. Besides this barrier, his "balancing of the equities" came out the same way. Hale's right to a fair trial outweighed the First Amendment right claimed by Father Mockaitis and Archbishop George.

The disappointed clergy appealed to us. A coalition of religious bodies joined in the appeal as friends of the court urging reversal. They included the United States Catholic Conference; the National Council of Churches of Christ in the U.S.A.; the Christian Legal Society; The Church of Jesus Christ of Latter-day Saints; Clifton Kirkpatrick, as Stated Clerk of the General Assembly of the Presbyterian Church (U.S.A.); The American Jewish Congress; The Commission on Social Action of Reform Judaism; The Baptist Joint Committee on Public Affairs; and the Evangelical Lutheran Church in America. The United States also intervened to defend the constitutionality of the Religious Freedom Restoration Act, a federal statute invoked by the appellants.

In the federal district court, Hale had been represented by a public defender. This lawyer did not appear at the appellate level, but the state, which shared Hale's position, referred to what the defendant had argued in the district court. Theodore R. Kulongonski, the attorney general of Oregon, conducted the appeal for Harcleroad.

The convention in appellate courts is that what is written in a brief or orally argued by a lawyer is attributed to the party represented by the lawyer. The reason for this convention is not clear, and it is sometimes misleading. In our case, it seemed particularly misleading because "Harcleroad," that is, the brief of the attorney-general, seemed not to have read Hale's confession. The brief writer searched hard to explain why the brief was defending an act that Harcleroad in person had told the district court was wrong. The brief writer came up with two reasons, both of them reasons that, if valid, would have helped Hale. One was that, in the death penalty phase of a capital case, Hale was entitled to

6. Owen M. Panner (1924–2018) was appointed a federal district judge in 1980 (chief judge 1984–90).

introduce mitigating evidence. The other reason was that in the trial itself, Hale was entitled to show that the prosecutor had gathered fruit from a poisonous tree and to move to exclude it. But how would Hale's confession have served either purpose? The admission of burglaries already admitted did not poison any later evidence. His false accusation against his co-defendant could only have served to aggravate his crime, not mitigate it. The bureaucratic exercise of inventing fallacious reasons for the state's position confirmed my sense that Harcleroad had no genuine interest to defend. Only the state's bureaucracy wanted to continue the litigation in order to insulate itself from the priests it saw as meddling with its business.

Hearing the appeal with me were David Thompson and Andy Kleinfeld.[7] Thompson had been appointed the same day I was and so I enjoyed seniority in respect to him and presided only because I was four years older. To the extent that religion might make a difference, I noted that he was Protestant. I also knew that he was the most equably-tempered of judges. Kleinfeld had been on the district court in Alaska and then moved to our court in 1991. Like Judge Boochever, he was originally from New York. His roots were Jewish. At no point in our hearing of the case did our three takes on it diverge: the taping was an outrage. I assigned the bench memo and the writing of the case to myself.

The most obvious federal law that had been breached by Harcleroad was the Religious Freedom Restoration Act, known by the acronym RFRA. The statute had come into effect in November 1993, approximately two and one-half years prior to the events in our case. The House had passed it unanimously, the Senate with only three dissents, and President Clinton had signed it into law. It was not only bipartisan legislation but the fruit of a broadly ecumenical religious coalition joined by such guardians of constitutional freedom as the American Civil Liberties Union.

RFRA was a pointed rebuke to an opinion that Justice Scalia had written for the Supreme Court in *Employment Division v. Smith*.[8] Scalia had said that, if a state enforced a general rule that had the effect of burden-

---

7. David R. Thompson (1930–2011) served on the Ninth Circuit from 1985 until 2011. Andrew J. Kleinfeld (born 1945) was a federal magistrate judge (1971–74) and district judge (1986–91), before he was appointed to the Ninth Circuit in 1991.

8. *Emp. Div., Dep't of Hum. Res. of Oregon v. Smith*, 494 U.S. 872 (1990)

ing a particular religion, the state did not violate the burdened believers' free exercise of religion. In Smith these believers had been state employees who participated in a Native American Indian religious ritual that treated peyote as a sacrament. The state of Oregon had acted constitutionally in firing them, the Supreme Court had said: the state could penalize drug-taking state employees. Now, in RFRA, Congress legislated that no government, federal or state, should substantially burden any person's exercise of religion unless the government could demonstrate its compelling interest in imposing the burden and showed that imposing it was "the least restrictive means" of furthering that compelling interest. It was evident that taping Hale's confession was not the least restrictive means of achieving the prosecutor's end. The ordinary means to achieve the prosecutor's goal was good police work. It was equally evident that the taping of confessions would make confessions odious. The burden imposed on the exercise of the Catholic religion was large. Harcleroad—I continue the convention that he speaks in the brief—did not attempt to dispute these points.

What Harcleroad did do was to attack the constitutionality of RFRA itself. The statute advanced the exercise of religion and was therefore, he argued, an establishment of religion prohibited by the First Amendment. He also invoked the tired language of Supreme Court jurisprudence on the subject to say that enforcement of RFRA necessitated an "excessive entanglement" of religion with government, because governments would have to make judgments about the burdens they were putting on specific religious practices.[9]

Harcleroad's claim of establishment of religion did not sit well with the history of our country. The creation of chaplaincies in Congress and the armed forces went back to its beginnings. The Internal Revenue Code advanced religion by giving exemptions to churches and deductions for gifts to churches. The draft laws had typically exempted various religious objectors to war. A host of federal laws would have to be thrown out if their benefit to religion was a serious stain on their constitutionality. As for entanglement with religion, RFRA no more entangled a government by making the government define a religious practice than the First Amendment itself did in requiring Congress and the courts to de-

9. The phrase "excessive government entanglement with religion" goes back to *Walz v. Tax Comm'n of City of New York*, 397 U.S. 664, 674 (1970).

termine what constituted a religion and to respect an exercise of it. You could not protect the free exercise of religion or limit governmental intrusion on it without saying something definite about what religion was and what constituted its practice. A good part of my opinion was devoted to destroying the establishment argument.

Harcleroad had, as a good lawyer should, a second string to his bow. Well aware of the *Smith* decision upholding Oregon law over the peyote users, religious though their ritual was, he maintained that here, too, were neutral Oregon statutes that trumped the religious claim. One statute, at least implicitly, authorized the interception and recording of conversations between inmates and all visitors except their attorneys. Another Oregon statute required the state to disclose to a criminal defendant all his statements recorded by the state. Another statute forbade the destruction of physical evidence. So Harcleroad was duty-bound to keep the tape and let it be used. Under *Smith*, there was no denial of religious freedom in enforcing these neutral laws. If RFRA went beyond the Supreme Court's reading of the First Amendment, Congress had acted unconstitutionally; RFRA was invalid.

Having recently written a book, *The Lustre Of Our Country*, examining the American experience of religious freedom, I was not persuaded by this line of attack.[10] In 1966, the Supreme Court had held in a famous civil rights case that Congress in enforcing the Constitution was not confined to the restrictions placed by the courts on the states.[11] The Fourteenth Amendment had given Congress the power and the responsibility to determine "whether and what legislation is needed" to secure the liberties that the Constitution guaranteed. I did not think that the Supreme Court would decide otherwise now. I did not appreciate the political currents that were inverting the meaning of "federalism" and under this banner reasserting what had once been called "States' rights" in resisting federal supervision.[12]

I wrote the opinion before RFRA had reached the Supreme Court. While our case was under our consideration, a RFRA case from Texas was making its way to Washington. Cert., as I noted, had even been granted. The Supreme Court was to use the case as the vehicle to repulse

---

10. *The Lustre of Our Country: The American Experience of Religious Freedom* (1998).

11. *Katzenbach v. Morgan*, 384 U.S. 641 (1966).

12. Judge Noonan discussed, critically, this shift in constitutional law in his 2002 book *Narrowing the Nation's Power: The Supreme Court Sides with the States.*

Congress's rebuke, holding it beyond the power of Congress to correct the Supreme Court's reading of the Constitution.[13] Harcleroad was on the right track with his contention that RFRA must be rejected as beyond the competence of Congress. My opinion on this point has retained a purely historical interest.

While I did not foresee what the Supreme Court would do, I was aware that we should provide for the unforeseen contingencies of constitutional law. I added a second ground for our decision: Harcleroad had violated the Fourth Amendment. To reach that conclusion I needed to show that Father Mockaitis had a reasonable expectation of privacy in his encounter with Hale. That expectation had its foundation in an Oregon statute and in our country's historical treatment of confession.

Oregon law, like the laws of all the states, created a "clergy-penitent privilege." A member of the clergy could not be examined on a communication made to him "in the member's professional character," unless the person making the communication gave permission.[14] The privilege was broader than sacramental confession but certainly sufficient to assure a priest that normally he could not be compelled to testify about a confession. Was this security to be subverted by technology?

The legal history of confession in this country began with a decision made by DeWitt Clinton as Mayor of New York City speaking for the Court of General Sessions in 1813.[15] Clinton rejected the prosecutor's attempt to force a priest to reveal the confession of a man accused of fencing stolen goods. The priest-penitent privilege had not been recognized in England after the Reformation. Clinton declared it essential to the free exercise of religion guaranteed by the First Amendment. "The sinner will not confess, nor will the priest receive his confession, if the veil of secrecy is removed: To decide that the minister shall promulgate what he receives in confession, is to declare that there shall be no penance; and this important branch of Roman Catholic religion would be thus annihilated."

---

13. *City of Boerne v. Flores*, 521 U.S. 507 (1997).

14. In at least one state, Virginia, the privilege apparently belongs to the clergyperson and the penitent's permission is not necessary. *See Nestle v. Commonwealth*, 470 S.E.2d 133, 137 (Va. App. 1996).

15. *People v. Phillips, reproduced in Privileged Communications to Clergymen*, 1 Cath. Law. 199 (1955). DeWitt Clinton (1769–1828) was a prominent political figure in the Founding Era and the Federalist candidate for president in 1812 despite his affiliation, before and after, with the Republican party.

Clinton drew an analogy between such state interference with Catholic practices and hypothetical interference with the Protestant practices of Baptism and the Lord's Supper: "Suppose that a decision of this court, or a law of the states should prevent the administration of one or both of these sacraments, would not the constitution be violated, and the freedom of religion be infringed? Every man who hears me will answer in the affirmative."

Blessed with immunity by this early pronouncement, sacramental confession was not thought of as a prosecutor's tool. All fifty states agreed. I could find no case reporting any intrusion upon it. A thesis at Boalt Hall, written by Jacob M. Yellin in 1983, had found none.[16] The Supreme Court of the United States in dicta in 1875 and again in 1980 had compared the confidences of the confessional to other recognized exceptions to the obligation to give testimony such as the privileges protecting confidences between attorney and client or between spouses.[17] In the face of that unbroken history, a priest hearing a confession had every reason to believe that what was said to him was inviolate.

Harcelroad met this argument by asserting that Hale did not have an expectation of privacy. It had been stipulated in the district court that Hale knew that his meetings with visitors other than his attorney were recorded by his jailers, and that he gave signals to visitors to warn them not to speak of matters that he wanted kept confidential. The content of his confession was such that he now wanted it preserved and used at his trial. The penitent, whose disclosures the privilege was meant to protect, wanted his disclosures made public.

It did strike me as paradoxical that the district attorney and the accused killer should be on the same side and that the privilege should be maintained when the intended beneficiary did not want it maintained. It did occur to me to ask myself if Hale had really made a sacramental confession. He was not a Catholic. As a baptized Christian, he was eligible under canon law to seek sacramental absolution, but he very well might have attached no meaning to it. Was the recording not a way of his denying guilt without taking the stand and subjecting himself to crossexamination? He seemed to have used his confession to set a trap for Har-

16. Jacob M. Yellin, *The History and Current Status of the Clergy-Penitent Privilege*, 23 Santa Clara L. Rev. 95 (1983).

17. *Totten v. United States*, 92 U.S. 105, 107 (1875); *Trammel v. United States*, 445 U.S. 40, 51 (1980).

cleroad, who he knew would tape him. Was the litigation before us over a pseudo-confession that should simply be allowed to enter Hale's own case as it now appeared in ours? Did the privilege no longer exist as to Hale?

Still, it was neither logically nor factually impossible for one party to a communication to have a reasonable expectation of privacy, which the law would protect, and the other party not to have one. Such was the case of any telephone caller, whose call, unknown to him, was taped by the one called. Father Mockaitis had expected privacy in order to be assured of a full confession by one presenting himself as a penitent. It was the priest's expectation of privacy that the prosecutor had violated. And he had violated it, according to the affidavit supporting the warrant for seizure, with the purpose of taking advantage of the religious rite's requirement of full disclosure by the penitent. The recording had not been a neutral application of a prison regulation but an entry into a private realm to exploit a private religious encounter.

Father Mockaitis's expectation of privacy in hearing confessions had been violated; so had Archbishop George's analogous expectation as to confessions in the archdiocese over which he presided. As the Fourth Amendment had been violated, so had the Civil Rights Act which provided redress for the deprivation of any right "secured by the Constitution and laws." We remanded to Judge Panner to issue an injunction banning Harcleroad from further violation of the Fourth Amendment by recording confidential communications to the clergy at the Lane Jail. We directed the award of attorney fees to which the plaintiffs were entitled under the Civil Rights Act. We did not order the destruction of the tape already made. The psychological burden that its preservation put on Father Mockaitis seemed little different from that inflicted by his remembering the incident. Hale did have the right to report what he had said in confession. If he wanted to use the recording, we would not now prevent it.

Hale was subsequently tried before a jury and convicted of the aggravated murder of the three victims. Kristin Bendele, fifteen years old, had been Hale's girlfriend. He had first sodomized her and then killed her with her current boyfriend, Brandon Williams. Patrick Finley appears to have been killed just because he was with them. Susbauer pleaded guilty to the murders, cooperated with the district attorney, and was sentenced to life imprisonment without the possibility of parole. Hale was sentenced to death.

In the year 2000, Hale, still on death row in Oregon, received unexpected publicity. An interview with him in prison and a large photograph of his face and head and another of him standing with his arms extended at his sides as on a cross appeared in advertisements run by United Colors of Benetton, the clothing company. Besides advertising the company's name, the ads were meant to promote the abolition of capital punishment. The details of Hale's crimes were not furnished. Nor in the interview did he express any regret. He had been nineteen at the time of the murders. He was now twenty-four. The interview with him conveyed the poverty of his existence in which, he said, all that he had to do was watch television. If this ad served its humanitarian purpose, it was by suggesting that this murderer was a human being. As of this writing, Hale is still on death row.

The Oregon legislature in 1997 amended Oregon's Evidence Code to provide that a member of the clergy could not be examined as to a confidential communication even though the person making the communication consented, "if, under the discipline or tenets of the member's church, denomination, or organization, the member has an absolute duty to keep the communication confidential." The amendments appeared to reflect consideration of our case. The legislature, however, made no provision as to recording the confidential communication. On that topic our decision continues to be the law outlawing such intrusions.

As to the other parties in the case, Father Mockaitis was awarded damages of $45,000. He is now in his thirty-fourth year of priesthood and is pastor of Queen of Peace Church in Salem, Oregon. In 2009, he published *The Seal,* an account of his experience and reflections on the case. Francis George is archbishop of Chicago and a cardinal.[18] Douglas Harcleroad served 25 years as district attorney of Lane County and nine more years as Lane County prosecutor. Conan Wayne Hale has not been executed. He is imprisoned on death row. [19]

---

18. Francis Cardinal George died in 2015. Father Timothy Mockaitis remains pastor at Queen of Peace Church.

19. As of August 2025, this remains true.

NINE

# Into the Maze[1]

IN APRIL 1992, THE FEDERAL GOVERNMENT took the first step toward sending James Joseph Smyth ("Jimmy") back to Northern Ireland. Smyth had been born in Belfast in 1954. In 1977, he was arrested while living with his parents and charged with the attempted murder of a prison guard. He was tried by a Diplock court, the special creation of British law for safeguarding security in Northern Ireland: No jury was provided. A judge made the decisions. The normal rules as to the rights of defendants were relaxed and there was no right of appeal.[2] He was convicted and sentenced to twenty years imprisonment in the Maze.

In 1983, in a spectacular jail delivery, thirty-eight prisoners escaped from the Maze, among them Smyth. He made his way to San Francisco, earned his living as a house painter, and married an American girl. Learning of his true identity and whereabouts, the British government asked the American authorities to seek his extradition. The process required application of a treaty and a hearing before the federal district

---

1. *Matter of Extradition of Smyth*, 72 F.3d 1433 (9th Cir. 1996).

2. The popularly-labeled Diplock courts were implemented pursuant to a 1973 act of Parliament and officially abolished in 2007. Lord Diplock (William John Kenneth Diplock, 1907–85) was a distinguished judge and the author of a report that was the basis for the 1973 legislation. The Maze (officially HM Prison Maze, and named for the electoral ward of Maze in which it was located) was a prison in Northern Ireland used from 1971 to 2000 to house prisoners whom the British government viewed as terrorists or paramilitary offenders.

court in San Francisco. Barbara Caulfield, a particularly able judge, was assigned the case.[3]

The focus in San Francisco was on what might happen to Smyth if he fell again into the hands of his old jailers or the security forces. The treaty required this focus. Extradition "shall not occur," the treaty declared, if the person proved that he would be "punished, detained or restricted in his personal liberty by reason of his race, religion, nationality or political opinions." The British, acting through the United States, presented four witnesses to testify that Smyth, if returned, would be merely incarcerated to serve his sentence. Smyth, represented by a federal public defender, presented twenty-two witnesses as to conditions in the Maze and the broader practices of discrimination by the authorities against Catholics in Northern Ireland. Most relevantly, he produced evidence as to the treatment of the escapees in the 1983 break who had been recaptured and returned to the Maze. They had been forced by the prison guards to run a gauntlet of biting dogs.

Smyth asked the court to order the British government to produce several official reports of misconduct by the Royal Ulster Constabulary, the security forces in Northern Ireland. The British declared that the reports were confidential. As to two of the documents—the Stalker-Sampson Reports of 1985 and the Stevens Inquiry of 1989—the British specifically claimed the privilege of "state secrets." Judge Caulfield found that the documents addressed the British government's "direct or indirect involvement" with murder, attempted murder, and other injuries to Catholic nationalists. Balancing the British position against Smyth's need for the documents, the judge decided to penalize the refusal to provide the documents. The penalty was a rebuttable presumption that Catholic Irish nationalists found guilty of offenses against prison officers were systematically subjected to retaliatory harm, physical intimidation, and death.

The presumption virtually assured the outcome. The British case was further hurt by the refusal of several of the British witnesses to answer questions on cross-examination. The district judge found the refusals to lessen the weight to be given their testimony. After five weeks of hearings, the district judge held that the presumption of retaliatory punish-

3. Barbara A. Caulfield (1947–2010) served as a district judge (1991–94) and then returned to private practice.

ment had not been refuted, and that, even without the benefit of the presumption, Smyth had proven that he would be punished both in prison and on release into the general population of Northern Ireland. On behalf of the British, the United States appealed to us.

Initially, I had no involvement. I was not on the panel. I have no information as to how it reached its decision. In a tone of patient reasonableness, the opinion for the panel reviewed the findings of Judge Caulfield and the meaning of the treaty before making a startling observation: "the rules of evidence and civil procedure that govern federal court proceedings do not apply in extradition hearings that are conducted under the authority of a treaty enacted pursuant to Article II." The observation was attributed to Judge Caulfield, but the panel made it its own.[4] The observation was startling in that we, the judges of the Ninth Circuit, possessed the judicial power of the United States that Article III created. If Judge Caulfield or we were not exercising that power, what were we doing? The implication of the language I have just quoted was that we were delegates of the Executive Branch, which, acting under Article II of the Constitution, had made the treaty and authorized the hearings that the treaty required.

The corollary of the startling observation was that the district court did not have any authority to provide a sanction for the British failure to supply the requested reports. The presumption in Smyth's favor had "improperly shifted the burden of proof from Smyth to the government in contravention of the treaty provision." Without the presumption, the panel said Smyth had failed to prove that he would be mistreated in prison because of his political or religious beliefs. The panel reversed

4. *Matter of Requested Extradition of Smyth*, 61 F.3d 711, 720 (9th Cir.), *amended*, 73 F.3d 887 (9th Cir. 1995). The court of appeals panel introduced the quoted language with the words "As the court recognized." Judge Caulfield's two published orders include related although not necessarily synonymous observations. *See Matter of Extradition of Smyth*, 826 F. Supp. 316, 321 (N.D. Cal. 1993) ("neither the Federal Rules of Civil or Criminal Procedure are directly applicable to these proceedings [but] both rules provide guidance to the court in the exercise of its inherent power"); *Matter of Requested Extradition of Smyth*, 863 F. Supp. 1137, 1139 (N.D. Cal. 1994) ("The parties to the proceedings agreed that the Federal Rules of Evidence do not apply in extradition proceedings."). The Ninth Circuit had previously stated that although there is no statutory basis for discovery orders in extradition proceedings, the presiding judge "has the right, under the court's 'inherent power,' to order such discovery procedures 'as law and justice require.'" *Quinn v. Robinson*, 783 F.2d 776, 817 n. 41 (9th Cir. 1986).

Judge Caulfield and remanded the case for her to enter an order allowing Smyth's extradition.

The panel opinion was filed July 27, 1995. I was at once struck by the anomalous nature of this proceeding, cast in judicial form but apparently work of an administrative nature. I continued to look into the case in August and then left the country to take up a fellowship at the Norwegian Institute of Higher Studies. From Oslo, on September 12 considering the case afresh far from day-to-day pressures, I sent to my colleagues a call to take Smyth's case en banc.

To insert oneself into another panel's case is a difficult operation, not lightly to be undertaken. In theory, the panel speaks for a court that includes all its judges. The decision of the panel binds all of us in the future. We have a responsibility for what the panel does. In practice, the panel judges are the only ones who have heard the oral argument. The author of the panel opinion has devoted more time to the case than any judge outside the panel can. When voting on the en banc takes place, the voters—all the regular judges of the entire court—have little time to enter into the briefs and may vote on inadequate consideration of the merits. For some judges, a panel opinion is presumptively correct, and they are loath to add to our work the extra burden of eleven members of the court sitting en banc to read new briefs and hear oral argument again.

The en banc process is also wrapped in a certain amount of mystery. The memos exchanged between the judges debating the need for an en banc are cloaked with the same confidentiality that attends the panel memoranda preceding a decision. The judges' work product is not to be exposed to the eyes of the public.

Less defensibly, the actual vote on an en banc call is kept secret. Why? The reason I have heard is that some judges fear that their vote will be read as a vote on the merits, whereas in fact they voted as they did for other reasons—say, they didn't find the case important enough. I have seen a judge close to tears at the thought that his en banc vote would be disclosed. Nonetheless, an en banc vote is a judicial act. Many judicial acts are not completely explained and are therefore misunderstood. But they should be subject to scrutiny. Secrecy here is a bad custom that only Congress can eliminate.

In obedience to our practice, I will not report the debate or the vote, except to note that my call was defeated. One avenue of expressing disagreement publicly remained: a dissent from the court's failure to take the case en banc. Dissent of this kind is an enlargement of the original intrusion. I can't say that it is looked on by my colleagues with favor, but I can say that nearly all of them have resorted to it when they have been disappointed on an en banc vote.

One may legitimately ask what the function of such a dissent is. A common quip is that it's a cert. petition prepared by the dissenters. It does bolster the cert. petition that the losers will file. It is also an outlet for frustration. We, the dissenters assert, do not endorse the opinion which our court has left in place. In Smyth, I wrote such a dissent and was joined by Judges Pregerson, Reinhardt, and O'Scannlain.[5] Judge Reinhardt wrote a separate dissent, joined by me and Pregerson and O'Scannlain. The number of judges publicly dissenting in this way should not be construed to equal the number of judges who had voted in favor of the en banc.

I began my dissent drawing attention to the panel acting as if it were an Article II court. In doing so, the panel had gone directly against the position of the First Circuit interpreting the same treaty.[6] Liberated from judicial precedent, the panel had engaged in factfinding, a function normally performed by the district judge. The panel declared: "the strongest evidence of post-return politically motivated mistreatment" was "that the guards yelled racist and religious epithets while mistreating Smyth's fellow Maze escapees." The phrase "racist epithets" was an atavistic echo of the colonial past. Race was not at issue. Nationality was.

The panel not only missed the point but severed the yelling of the epithets from the abuse that accompanied it, the infliction of bodily injury on the returned prisoners by attacking guard dogs. Overlooking the attack, the panel also omitted Judge Caulfield's finding "that the same guards, who had staged the dog attack, left the prisoners' wounds unattended," they had engaged in a cover-up, and had been unpunished. They were 'a continued presence' at the prison."

The panel had added its own finding of fact by declaring Smyth to be a member of the IRA. To be a member was a crime under British law. The government had sought to introduce evidence to show Smyth to be a member, but Judge Caulfield had excluded it. There was nothing in the record to support the panel's gratuitous assertion.

---

5. Stephen R. Reinhardt (1931–2018) served on the Ninth Circuit (1980–2018); Diarmuid F. O'Scannlain (born 1937) was appointed to that court in 1986.

6. *In re Extradition of Howard*, 996 F.2d 1320 (1st Cir. 1993).

When the panel's attention was drawn to this gross error, the panel corrected it, grudgingly. They now spoke of "the IRA of which Smyth is reputedly a member." Who reputed him to be one? The panel did not say. Reputation is a fact. Where was this fact established? Without a basis, the panel gave Smyth a reputation for membership in an organization that was not only criminal but regarded with fear and loathing by many in Northern Ireland. The fact found by the panel would not be without significance to Smyth on his return to the Maze.

The panel had thrown out Judge Caulfield's presumption in favor of Smyth after the government's failure to comply with its discovery orders. It was hard to see how the treaty required the district court to give up its ability to enforce its orders. Only if one assumed that an Article II court should be a tame instrument of the Executive Branch was the panel's ruling on this point defensible.[7]

---

7. In his dissent from the court's refusal to grant a rehearing en banc, Judge Noonan discussed at greater length his constitutional objection to the panel's actions:

> The panel acted as an Article II court reviewing the decision of an Article II court. This fundamental misconception tainted all its deliberations. The appropriate remedy for this mistake is vacation of the court's judgment so that the court may address all the issues aware that it is performing the duties of an Article III tribunal.
>
> [In doing so,] the panel took upon itself a kind of political balancing appropriate for the Executive Branch and inappropriate for the Judicial Branch. The panel's misconception of itself as an Article II court no doubt accounts for this exercise in political wisdom. The posture in which the panel has put the case actually serves to underscore the proper responsibilities in these proceedings of the Executive Branch. The United Kingdom is not a party before this court. It is the United States, represented by the Department of Justice, that has interpreted the Treaty, sought Smyth's extradition, and appealed Judge Caulfield's order denying it. In making these significant decisions the Executive Branch has exercised discretion, a discretion not only affected by legal considerations but by political considerations. The Executive Branch has necessarily had its eye on relations between the United Kingdom and the United States. If, as appears likely, Smyth seeks a writ of certiorari from the Supreme Court of the United States, the Executive Branch must again exercise a discretion which is both legal and political in determining whether to defend the judgment of the panel or to concede error and accept the reasoned judgment of the district court.

72 F.3d at 1434, 1437–38.

Judge Reinhardt in his separate dissent stated:[8]

> To say that Smyth must prove that he will be subjected to additional punishment solely on account of political beliefs and not because he committed a particular crime is, according to the panel, "a difficult burden"; in fact, it is an impossible one. The panel's conclusion results from its misinterpretation of the Treaty. It creates a false dichotomy, one that is wholly unreal. In the black and white, all or nothing, world of the panel's opinion, there is the crime and the political opinion and never the twain shall meet. The truth however is that the two are inextricably linked, and thus inseparable.
>
> . . .
>
> In the case before us, the group identified as subject to systematic persecution is not as broad as the Jews in Germany; it is not all Irish Catholic nationals. Rather, it is a subset of that group: it is all Irish Catholic nationals believed to have committed certain crimes that are politically motivated. Because Smyth is a member of that subset, evidence of how his fellow members are systematically treated would be, as in a deportation case, highly relevant to how Smyth will be treated. While evidence of widespread retaliation against Catholic Irish republicans generally would not necessarily be sufficient, one would think that the panel would at least have recognized that such evidence is most probative as to any individual in Smyth's circumstances.

Despite our published dissents, the Supreme Court denied Smyth's petition for certiorari. He was turned over to the British authorities, brought back to the Maze, incarcerated, and beaten.[9] Less than two years later, the Good Friday accords of April 10, 1998 brought peace to Northern Ireland. The political prisoners of the Maze were released, among them Jimmy Smyth.

8. 72 F.3d at 1443, 1441–42.

9. *See* https://www.sfgate.com/news/article/ex-s-f-resident-says-irish-jailers-roughed-him-up-2846629.php. The British government denied Smyth's claim that he was beaten.

TEN

# The Heat Machine[1]

THE THERMOVISION 210, MADE AND MARKETED BY Agema Infrared Systems as Agema 210, is described by its maker in the following terms: "For law enforcement agencies and security organizations it provides a state-of-the-art means of extending operational capabilities and securing hard evidence not possible before. And it does it unobtrusively, noiselessly and immediately, requiring a minimum of operator training and effort." As to "Interior Surveillance," the company's sales brochure goes on to say: "With a field view of 8 degrees by 16 degrees, the 210, properly positioned, can monitor activity in critical rooms or large facilities, once again providing a permanent time-tagged record when connected to a VCR."

The Agema 210—a "gun" in the argot of *Time*—was deployed on January 16, 1992, by Sergeant Dan Haas from his car on Rhododendron Drive in Florence, Oregon. A member of a federal investigative team,[2] Haas was parked near the home of Danny Lee Kyllo, one of three units in a triplex. Within ten minutes Hass had a reading on the Agema of a much larger emission of heat from the roof and one wall of Kyllo's home than from the other two units. The time was 3:20 A.M., an unusual time for such heat to be generated. The Agema reading confirmed investigators' belief that Kyllo was growing marijuana. A report of the emissions was included, along with other bits of suspicious facts, in support of a

1. Citations to the opinions filed at the various decision points in this case's complicated history are in footnotes below.

2. At that time, Daniel Haas was a staff sergeant in the Oregon Army National Guard.

federal request for a warrant to search Kyllo's home. A federal magistrate issued the warrant. A marijuana grow was found.

Kyllo was indicted for manufacturing marijuana. He pleaded guilty with a condition: that his plea was revoked if he prevailed on his motion to suppress the evidence against him. The district judge, Helen J. Frye,[3] denied his motion and sentenced him to five years and three months imprisonment. Kyllo appealed to us.

When I came to the court, I had little enthusiasm for freeing defendants because the police had violated the Fourth Amendment. As Benjamin Cardozo had phrased it, the defendant should not escape "because the constable had blundered."[4] In my first year on the court, sitting with civil libertarians Steve Reinhardt and Bill Canby I had written a spirited dissent against letting go a major drug distributor because "the brave agents," as I called them, had thought it necessary to pounce upon him without a warrant.[5]

Socialization or familiarity with the practices of the police had eroded this layman's skepticisms about enforcing the Constitution by reversing the conviction of a criminal. I had come to see how hard otherwise it was to restrain official zeal and how essential it was to preserve an area of privacy. In 1997, when I heard Kyllo's appeal argued in Portland, I was open to a solidly-based invocation of the Constitution's prohibition of searches without a warrant.

Our first reaction to the case was to see if the Orwellian dangers suggested by Kyllo's appeal existed. Could the machine report the heat generated by sexual intercourse? We remanded to Judge Frye for the necessary factfinding. She reported that the dangers were imaginary. The Agema 210 was a less perceptive observer than its advertising suggested. What it reported were comparative temperatures. The case came back to us. Meanwhile, Judge Frye had reduced Kyllo's sentence from 5¼ years to one month plus probation.

My reaction now was to affirm Judge Frye's denial of the motion to suppress. My colleagues were Michael Daly Hawkins, a former United

---

3. Helen Jackson Frye (1930–2011) was a district judge from 1980 until her death.

4. *People v. Defore*, 150 N.E. 585, 587 (N.Y. 1926).

5. *United States v. Alvarez*, 810 F.2d 879, 891 (9th Cir. 1987) (Noonan, Cir. J., dissenting). The text abbreviates the language of Judge Noonan's opinion, which referred to "the arresting agents" as "these brave men" in the same paragraph.

States Attorney in Phoenix, a thoughtful middle-of-the-roader, and Bob Merhige, a district judge in Richmond, Virginia.[6] Merhige, a Brooklynite, had migrated to Virginia and had been on the district court in Richmond during the battles over school desegregation. He was a civil libertarian, increasingly restive under the heavy hand of the Fourth Circuit and glad to join us in California as a visitor. Both Hawkins and Merhige, fairminded men, joined me in rejecting Kyllo's claim that the heat machine had unconstitutionally searched his home.

I was assigned the opinion and tried to write it. As the expression goes, it would not write. Such changes of mind after the judges have conferred are not unknown although not usual. In this case, I credit one influence on me to have been my law clerk, John Lundin.

John Lundin was a man in his forties, unusually mature to be a law clerk. He had enlisted in the United States Army as a private and risen though the ranks to major. He had then resigned and attended Columbia Law School. Lou Henkin, a pillar of the school, wrote me that Lundin was "one of our OWLS," i.e., Older and Wiser Law Students. So I found him. In this case, he told me of his experience with heat machines in the army. They were effective agents on border patrol. He suggested they were search machines. I changed my vote and on November 21, 1997 sent Judges Hawkins and Merhige an opinion I hoped they would accept.

On February 27, 1998, I prodded my colleagues with a two-sentence email:

> What is happening? If we do not decide soon, I'll be confusing the Agema with the Enigma.

Judge Merhige telephoned me at once to say "I have vacillated on this case as I never have before." But he went on to send me a new opinion which he said "had its genesis" in mine.

It was one of those diplomatic crises not unusual on appellate panels. He was much my senior in age and experience, but he was from outside the circuit and I had already written what I thought was a good opinion. I decided that I should graciously join in what he wrote. No need to in-

6. Michael D. Hawkins (born 1945) joined the Ninth Circuit in 1994. Robert R. Merhige, Jr. (1919–2005) was a judge in the Eastern District of Virginia (1967–98).

sist here on my own phrasing. On March 25, 1998, 2–1, we held the Fourth Amendment to have been violated.[7]

Predictably, given the division of the court, the government asked for rehearing by the panel and rehearing by the court en banc. Judge Merhige and I rejected this request, but before Judge Hawkins had voted on it and therefore before we could file the order denying the request, Judge Merhige retired from the bench to enter private practice. I sent a message to Mike Hawkins suggesting that as we were now tied, 1–1, the government's petition was denied. He properly replied that a new third judge should be drawn to resolve the matter. Accordingly, by lot, Judge Brunetti was selected.[8] As very often is the case when you are familiar with the judge, you can guess how he will vote. It is not cynicism but experience that breeds such guesses. I knew at once that I had lost my majority.

Kyllo objected to the procedure. When a judge was replaced on a panel, a new panel was created. It could no longer "rehear" the case. It was a new panel. Rehearing was simply not possible. At one level of realism, this argument made sense. But precedent was against it, as well as the practical consideration that a fluke should not prevent the normal practice of taking a second look. Kyllo's objection failed.[9]

The Agema 210, Judge Hawkins wrote for the new majority, "did not literally or figuratively penetrate the walls of the Kyllo residence."[10] The machine had merely read emissions from the outside surface of the houses. Whatever expectation Kyllo had as to the privacy of the interior, he had none as to the surface from which the waste heat radiated. He had failed to show a subjective expectation of privacy, and he had equally failed to show that society accepted a standard that prohibited the government from measuring hot spots in a house; no intimate details of Kyllo's life were thereby revealed. The authoritative definition by the Su-

---

7. *United States v. Kyllo*, 140 F.3d 1249, 1250 (9th Cir. 1998).

8. Melvin T. Brunetti (1933–2009) served on the Ninth Circuit from 1985 until 1999.

9. The propriety of the Ninth Circuit's highly unusual practice in this regard was debated in later cases, *Carver v. Lehman*, 558 F.3d 869 (9th Cir. 2009), and *Perez v. City of Roseville*, 926 F.3d 511, 528 (9th Cir. 2019), and squarely challenged as unlawful by retired federal judges in a Supreme Court amicus brief. The Court ultimately declined to review a Federal Circuit decision following the Ninth Circuit practice. *Novartis Pharms. Corp. v. HEC Pharm Co.*, 143 S. Ct. 1748 (2023).

10. *United States v. Kyllo*, 190 F.3d 1041 (9th Cir. 1999).

preme Court stated that a search occurred when the government breached "an expectation of privacy that society is prepared to consider reasonable."[11] Kyllo did not have the expectation. Society was not prepared to consider such an expectation reasonable. No search, therefore, had happened.

In reply, I started with the same definition of a search but added to it another proposition from the Supreme Court: "The sanctity of the home is not to be disputed."[12] A forbidden search could occur even when no trespass into the home was made. The closest analogy to the Agema 210 was a telescope that unknown to the homeowner could see into a house and detect objects not visible to the naked eye. The Second Circuit, our respected peer in New York, had held the use of such a telescope to be a search.[13] No principled distinction existed between reading reflections of light and reading emissions of heat. Amplification of the senses by technology in each case defeated the homeowner's expectation of privacy as to what he was doing in his home.

Was society prepared to protect this expectation? I noted a tension between the desirability of suppressing crime and the barrier that the Fourth Amendment raised. To my mind, the Fourth Amendment already embodied society's preference for the inviolability of the home except in the most exigent circumstances where no time existed to seek a warrant from a magistrate.

The majority had stressed that no intimate details of Kyllo's life could be scrutinized by the Agema 210. I poked fun at this dependence on the deficiencies of the machine. Because what was revealed was not personal or a specific activity, the majority held that no search was being performed. To the contrary, I suggested that was like holding that there was no search if the governmental intruder was a blind policeman.

I also noted that personal and specific activities would register on the Agema 210. "A variety of heat-producing activities," I wrote, "can take place within the walls of a home. As to such of these activities as are innocent, no one doubts that society views the expectation of privacy as reasonable—for example, the use of a sauna in a sauna room; the making of ceramics in a kiln in the basement; the hothouse cultivation of

11. *United States v. Jacobsen*, 466 U.S. 109, 122 (1984).

12. *Segura v. United States*, 468 U.S. 796, 810 (1984).

13. *United States v. Taborda*, 635 F.2d 131 (2d Cir. 1980).

orchids, poinsettias or other plants in a domestic greenhouse. Any of such activities can cause the emission of heat from the home which the Agema 210 can detect. The activity will be reported as well as where it is taking place. That is the present, not potential, intrusion of privacy which the Agema 210 can effect."

The new majority's opinion was filed September 9, 1999. Kyllo had 14 days to ask for rehearing. On September 15, his lawyer, Kenneth Lerner, who had maintained his case with skill and spirit, asked for an extension of time. He had been "deprived of the full 14 days because of his unavailability during the Jewish High Holidays," and "the press of other cases and preexisting commitments" made it impossible "to file a coherent petition for rehearing in the normal time allotted." The panel granted the extra week he asked for.

Kyllo now petitioned for rehearing by the panel and for rehearing en banc. I remained a minority on the panel and did not take the initiative to ask my colleagues on the court to go en banc. It's been my observation that if a dissent does not stir anther judge to request an en banc, the dissenter wastes his time in asking for it. On December 14, 1999, Kyllo's two petitions were denied with no judge seeking review by an en banc. Kyllo had one last possibility; that the Supreme Court would grant cert. On September 26, 2000, it did.[14]

Argument before the Supreme Court took place February 20, 2001. A divided court reversed the circuit on June 11.[15] The division was as remarkable as the result. Justice Scalia, writing the opinion, was joined by Justices Souter, Thomas, Ginsburg, and Breyer. Justice Stevens, dissenting, was joined by Chief Justice Rehnquist and Justices O'Connor and Kennedy. These were combinations not likely to occur.

For Justice Stevens, there had not been an invasion of Kyllo's home but an inference drawn from emissions off the walls. Heat waves, like smells, entered the public domain "if and when they leave a building." Expectation that they would remain private was implausible and surely not one that society was prepared to recognize as reasonable. Justice Stevens concluded that Justice Scalia was anticipating dangers from new technology, not ruling on "the fairly primitive thermal images" used against Kyllo.

---

14. *Kyllo v. United States*, 530 U.S. 1305 (2000).
15. *Kyllo v. United States*, 533 U.S. 27 (2001).

Justice Scalia disputed Justice Stevens' assertion that the Agema 210 did not learn about the interior of the house. The machine obtained information about the relative heat of different rooms. Its action was as much an invasion of privacy as the action of an eavesdropping device that picked up sound waves reaching the exterior of a phone booth. The distinction between an inference and an invasion, Justice Scalia observed, was equally unsustainable. The activation of a beeper the police had planted in a can of ether had, in another case, led the police to infer that the ether was in the house: the police were held to have made an unconstitutional search.[16] Finally, noting that the dissenters would disapprove of technology revealing intimate details in the home, Justice Scalia observed that no principled distinction could be drawn between intimate and nonintimate details. In the home all details were intimate because the home was "safe from prying government eyes." Even the can of ether in the beeper case had been held to be protected from detection. The Agema 210 itself could detect at what hour each night the lady of the house took her daily sauna. Many, Justice Scalia observed, would think that an intimate fact. And using more sophisticated equipment, how could the police know in advance whether they would be picking up details that everyone would consider intimate? Justice Scalia's majority moved, in effect, to throttle the Orwellian monster before it grew.

The case was returned to us, and we returned it to the district court, which suppressed the evidence and vacated Kyllo's plea of guilty.

From start to finish the case had taken over ten years. A total of seven judges (five on the Supreme Court and two on the circuit) had found the technology to violate the Fourth Amendment and seven judges (four on the Supreme Court, two on the circuit, and one in the district court) had held that it did not. The arguments on each side were such that reasonable persons might disagree and did. Enjoying the luxury of a long time in which to consider the matter and argue about it, the judges had slowly come to a conclusion. If they erred, they had erred on the side of the liberty of the individual.

16. *United States v. Karo*, 468 U.S. 705 (1984).

ELEVEN

# Finding Alexis Barrera-Echavarria[1]

IN THE SPRING OF 1980, FIDEL CASTRO carried out the unusual idea of depositing on the shores of the United States over 120,000 Cubans. "You want to help the people dissatisfied with me," he said in effect. "Here they are, help them." Many of these so-called Mariel Cubans were regarded as undesirables in Cuba. Among them was Alexis Barrera-Echavarria, who had been awaiting trial in Havana as a pickpocket. On May 29, 1980, he arrived in Key West, Florida.

Arrested on arrival by the authorities, Barrera, like most of the Mariels, was paroled into the United States—that is, he was not admitted as a legal visitor or immigrant, but conditionally released from custody with his final status left for determination. This ambiguous position meant that in the eyes of American law he was not within the country. As an en banc court was to express it, he was not "deemed to be present on United States territory." [2]

Barrera was not deemed to be present, but he made his presence known. In July 1982, he was arrested for robbery of a woman's jewelry at the point of a pistol. He was sentenced to jail for 236 days in Florida but within the year had been released. In May 1983, he was convicted of burglary of a building and received a two-year sentence in state prison. In February 1985, still imprisoned, he received a notice of detention from the Immigration and Naturalization Service. At the end of his state

1. *Barrera-Echavarria v. Rison*, 21 F.3d 314, 315 (9th Cir. 1994).

2. *Barrera-Echavarria v. Rison*, 44 F.3d 1441, 1450 (9th Cir. 1995) (en banc) ("excludable aliens are deemed under the entry doctrine not to be present on United States territory").

sentence, he was taken into federal custody. When we heard his case on appeal in 1994, he had been in such custody at the request of the INS for over eight years. His time had been spent in Bastrop, a medium security institution, and in three high security penitentiaries, Atlanta, Lompoc, and Leavenworth.

Incarceration in Lompoc in 1990 gave Barrera the opportunity to seek habeas corpus in the federal district court in Los Angeles.[3] On October 12, 1993, District Judge David V. Kenyon granted the writ,[4] requiring Attorney General Janet Reno to release Barrera from prison to a halfway house or some other form of supervised release. The government appealed. While the appeal was pending, the government moved Barrera to Leavenworth in Kansas. The move did not moot the appeal.

In the argument before us, in February 1994, Barrera was immensely aided by a first class Los Angeles law firm furnishing him free counsel. Karen N. Fredriksen and Mark D. Kemper of Gibson, Dunn & Crutcher acted pro bono on his behalf, providing the kind of help that most aliens need in their encounters with the law, but few receive. Lucas Guttentag and Ann Parrent of New York City joined them in appearing for several amici, including the ACLU, the American Immigration Law Center, the Asian American Legal Defense Fund, and the Mexican American Legal Defense Fund. From the breadth of the coalition the case's importance to immigration law could be inferred. Emily Anne Rudford acted for the Attorney General. The "us" before whom the argument was held were James Browning, now retired as chief but still an active judge at seventy-five; Joseph T. Sneed, a man of deeply conservative instincts, once Deputy Attorney General under President Nixon; and me.[5]

Barrera had been a problem for the government. The INS had approved him for parole in 1990 but had not found a halfway house willing to take him. In 1992, he was paroled to such a house run by the Public Health Service. Six months later, he was accused of sexually assaulting another resident; the case did not go to trial but Barrera was returned to prison. It was a matter of dispute whether he was a homosexual who might force himself on others or whether, because of his small size, he

3. Lompoc is in California.

4. David V. Kenyon (1930–2015) was a California municipal court and then superior court judge (1971–80) before serving as a federal district judge (1980–97).

5. Joseph T. Sneed III (1920–2008) was briefly deputy attorney general in 1973, and served on the Ninth Circuit from then until his death.

was the victim of homosexual attacks. The government noted his failure to get or keep parole without establishing that his setbacks had been warranted. The government referred vaguely to its efforts to "secure his repatriation" without submitting any specific information as to what it had attempted as to Barrera. The government seemed to be sure that Cuba was not about to take him back and that no other country would accept him. In the government's view, only the continued denial of parole kept a dangerous criminal out of the community.

The government's principal authority for doing what it did was *Mezei*, a case decided by the Supreme Court in 1953.[6] Ignatz Mezei, born offshore in Gibraltar, had lived in the United States 24 years and had acquired the status of a resident alien. At age 51, he stayed in two Communist countries for a period of about two years. On his return, he was intercepted by the INS and interned at Ellis Island; the reason for his internment was a secret undisclosed by the Attorney General. His status was that of an excluded alien, legally not present in the United States. The Second Circuit, 2–1, held he was entitled to habeas. Learned Hand, dissenting, compared Mezei to the Flying Dutchman, a man without a country and without any right to remain here.[7] The Supreme Court, 5–4, followed Hand, the most respected circuit judge in the country. Dissenting, Justice Jackson, the prosecutor of the Nazi leaders at Nuremberg, compared the government's action of confining Mezei on information undisclosed to him or any tribunal to the practice of protective custody by which the Nazis imprisoned those they "expected" to commit treason. He quoted Hermann Goering defending the process, and he ended the dissent, "No one can make me believe we are that far gone."[8]

6. *Shaughnessy v. United States ex rel. Mezei*, 345 U.S. 206 (1953).

7. *United States ex rel. Mezei v. Shaughnessy*, 195 F.2d 964, 971 (2d Cir. 1952) (L. Hand, Cir. J., dissenting).

8. *See Mezei*, 345 U.S. at 225 n. 8 (Jackson, J., dissenting) ("Hermann Goering... made the following statements: '[T]hose who had committed some act of treason against the new state, or those who might be proved to have committed such an act, were naturally turned over to the courts. The others, however, of whom one might expect such acts, but who had not yet committed them, were taken into protective custody, and these were the people who were taken to concentration camps.... Likewise, if for political reasons... someone was taken into protective custody, that is, purely for reasons of state, this could not be reviewed or stopped by any court.'"); *id.* at 228 (Jackson, J., dissenting) ("It is inconceivable to me that this measure of simple justice and fair dealing [providing judicial process] would menace the security of this country. No one can make me believe that we are that far gone.").

A year after this indication of the executive branch's power, the government released Mezei and he returned home to Buffalo.

Why didn't *Mezei* govern Barrera's case? For two reasons, I thought—a difference in the conditions in which Mezei was held and a difference in the duration of his confinement. At Ellis Island, Mezei slept in a dormitory and spent the day in the great Passenger Hall. He was free to read and write as he chose. Most striking of all, his day-to-day companions were foreigners waiting for admission, not convicted felons. In contrast, the three high security penitentiaries that had housed Barrera entailed severe conditions for their inmates. Leavenworth, where Barrera was now residing, had capacity for 951 prisoners and a prison population of over 1,500. It was encircled by a massive wall with gun towers at each corner. The Bureau of Prisons described it as a "correctional" institution, whose inhabitants were "offenders." The Bureau's announced aim in treating these offenders was "a balance between punishment, deterrence, incapacitation, and rehabilitation."[9] No mention was made by the Bureau of any special purpose in its treatment of an excluded alien. As for time, Mezei had been held for over two years when his case was heard, in distinction to the over eight years of Barrera's federal imprisonment. Duration made a difference.

To my mind, not only was *Mezei* distinguishable. Once it was acknowledged that the penitentiaries were places of punishment, the case was over. The government might maintain the fiction that Barrera was not in the United States even when it held him in the middle of Kansas. The government could not maintain that it was not punishing him. Besides the Bureau of Prisons' own statement of purpose, the facts were incontestable. Immurement in an isolated fortress; deprivation of choice as to companions, use of leisure time, and sexual opportunities; exposure to sexual assault—these conditions were not punishment! No one could maintain that. Once punishment was conceded, precedent spoke. No person may be punished by the United States without a conviction following a trial. So the United States Supreme Court had held in *Wong Wing* in 1896.[10] Nothing had altered that fundamental principle. The principle was protection for everyone who was a person. The government did not allege that Barrera was not a person.

---

9. Federal Bureau of Prisons, *Federal Correctional Facilities* 3 (1991).

10. *Wong Wing v. United States*, 163 U.S. 228, 229 (1896).

Branch" supervision over powers belonging to the executive. Justice Scalia maintained that there was no constitutional difficulty to be avoided. The inadmissible aliens were claiming a constitutional right to be in this country. They had, he wrote, no right to be here. But with this decision aliens admitted to the United States could not be imprisoned at the pleasure of the INS.

The question remained whether an alien not admitted to the United States could also obtain release. In August 2002, the Ninth Circuit, acting through Judge Margaret McKeown, held he could.[20] The case was that of Lin Guo Xi, a Chinese man captured by the Coast Guard off the coast of Guam as he operated a boat smuggling other aliens into American territory.[21] In 1997, Xi had been sentenced to six months imprisonment for his smuggling activity. The INS had then imprisoned him and had unsuccessfully tried to arrange his return to China. A middle-of-the-road liberal, McKeown was joined by Judge Ronald Gould, an independent thinker.[22]

Judge Pamela Rymer filed a spirited dissent:[23] *Mezei* and *Barrera* were still good law. The Supreme Court in *Zadydas* and *Ma* had addressed only the cases of resident aliens. Justice Breyer had written that *Zadydas* left "no unprotected spot in the Nation's armor."[24] Judge Rymer said that the McKeown majority created one. But the majority replied that it must interpret the statute the same way for resident and inadmissible aliens; the words could not mean different things in different situations. Moreover, not only had *Zadydas* undercut *Barrera* but the immigration statute now at issue was technically different, so that *Barrera* was no longer binding precedent in the circuit. Eight years after the 10–1 en banc decision, *Barrera* was history.

Still, the Supreme Court had not spoken. Were Judges McKeown and Gould or Judge Rymer right? In a follow-up, Judge Owen Panner applied *Xi* to grant habeas to Sergio Suarez Martinez, a Mariel Cuban

---

20. M. Margaret McKeown (born 1951) was appointed to the Ninth Circuit in 1998.

21. *Xi v. INS*, 298 F.3d 832 (9th Cir. 2002).

22. Robert M. Gould (born 1946) was appointed to the Ninth Circuit in 1999.

23. Pamela A. Rymer (1941–2011) was a district judge (1983–89) before her service on the Ninth Circuit (1989–2011).

24. *Xi*, 298 F.3d at 842 (Rymer, Cir. J., dissenting) (quoting *Zadvydas*, 533 U.S. at 695).

imprisoned in Oregon.[25] The circuit—Chief Judge Mary Schroeder and Judges Mike Hawkins and Wally Tashima—affirmed in a summary order citing *Xi* and finding no issue worth the writing of a published opinion.[26] Then, nemesis, it might have appeared, struck. The Bush Administration sought cert. Another Mariel Cuban, Daniel Benitez, had been convicted of grand theft, two armed burglaries, aggravated battery, and various offenses involving guns. The INS had arranged for his imprisonment when his state sentences ended. A federal district judge in Northern Florida denied his habeas petition. The Eleventh Circuit agreed, citing Judge Rymer's dissent in *Xi*.[27] Now there was not just a division among judges but among circuits. Cert. was granted in both cases.

Once again, the Supreme Court may have surprised the lookers-on who go by cliche.[28] Justice Scalia, who had dissented so sharply in *Zadydas*, wrote the opinion of the Court. The statute must be given the same meaning in the case of inadmissible aliens as in the case of resident aliens. The reading given the statute in *Zadydas* must be followed. Only Justice Thomas, joined by the Chief, dissented. *Barrera* was finally buried.

This decision, entitled *Clark v. Suarez Martinez,* was issued on January 12, 2005. When I learned of it, I thought that someone should tell Barrera. For all I knew he was still in Leavenworth. If he did not have a lawyer, he might not have heard of it or understood its consequences. I asked my law clerk, Brian O'Donoghue, to contact the Bureau of Prisons and find out.

Brian found a probation officer who undertook to look for him. By February 14, 2005, the probation officer had determined Barrera's date of birth, his alien registration number, his FBI number and "some other information" that might be helpful. On February 22, 2005, the officer had found him.

---

25. On Judge Panner, see page 65 & n. 6.

26. *Suarez Martinez v. Ashcroft,* 2003 WL 23892563 (9th Cir. 2003).

27. *Benitez v. Wallis,* 337 F.3d 1289, 1290 (11th Cir. 2003).

28. *Clark v. Suarez Martinez,* 543 U.S. 371 (2005).

At a time we were not told, Barrera had been paroled from prison by the INS. He had then committed a crime in California. He was currently beginning to serve his sentence at the Sierra Conservation Center. His earliest release date from his state sentence was August 26, 2006.[29]

---

29. It is unclear what happened with Mr. Barrera after this date. *See also* John T. Noonan, Jr., *The Heart of A Catholic Law School*, 23 U. Dayton L. Rev. 7, 12 (1997):

> For eight years a man had been imprisoned by federal authorities—a man who had never been federally convicted of any federal offense, who had committed no federal crime. By a writ as powerful and as magical as the *lettres de cachet* by which the king of France used to imprison disfavored subjects, an anonymous official of the Immigration Service was able to effectively incarcerate a man without trial in a free country, a country where due process of law is the fundamental guarantee of justice.
>
> Why was it done? Because the Immigration Service did not have the imagination to devise a way of returning Barrera to Cuba where Castro declared him barred, and no other country would take him. How was it defended? It was not imprisonment, but only a detention—the detention of an alien who had entered the country illegally, indeed who in the fiction of the Immigration Service had never entered the country. The bureaucratic mind loves fictions. A fiction is a wonderful management tool: It can always be manipulated. Barrera at the time of his lawsuit was in the middle of America in Leavenworth, Kansas, enclosed by a massive wall with gun towers at each corner. But he was not in the country, he was not imprisoned, he was merely detained in space metaphorically outside the United States.
>
> This story has an unhappy ending. The federal district court freed Barrera by a writ of habeas corpus. Our panel of the Ninth Circuit affirmed. But an en banc court, adhering to apparent Supreme Court precedent, reversed. The fiction that Barrera was not in the country was said to be "conceptually defensible." (What fiction is not?). The attorney general was found to have statutory authority to order the so-called detention (another fiction was accepted). International law condemning "prolonged arbitrary detention" was brushed aside. Barrera was kept in his cell. He will remain in his cell until relations with Cuba improve to the point of permitting his return, or he may remain until he dies, a prisoner of the Immigration Service in perpetuity, incarcerated without trial, held forever by the force of convenient fictions.

TWELVE

# Losing Robert Alton Harris[1]

ON JULY 5, 1978, ROBERT ALTON HARRIS and his brother Daniel set out to steal a stranger's automobile so that they could have a getaway car when they robbed the San Diego Trust and Savings Bank. In a parking lot directly across from the bank two boys sat in a green Ford, eating hamburgers. Robert Harris pulled out a pistol and told the boys to drive to a fire trail near Mirama Lake. Daniel followed in his brother's car.

At the foot of the trail, the cars were parked. The boys were forced to walk up the trail at gunpoint. Part way up, Robert Harris shot one of the boys, John Mayeski, aged 15, in the back. He put a second bullet in his head. The other boy, Michael Baker, aged 16, ran and hid in the brush. Robert Harris pursued him. He begged for his life. Harris shot him four times. Robert returned to John Mayeski and shot him again in the head.

The Harrises went back to Robert's house. He ate the rest of the boys' unfinished hamburgers. He laughed at his brother for not having the stomach to join him in the meal.

The Harrises then robbed the bank and returned to Robert's house with the proceeds of the robbery. A witness followed them to the house and called the police. They were arrested a little after 1:00 in the afternoon. At 4:00 Daniel informed police of the murders and at 6:30 put the blame on Robert. At 7:00 Robert confessed. At midnight he was examined by a psychiatrist retained by the state, Wait Griswold.

---

1. *Harris v. Vasquez*, 901 F.2d 724, 725 (9th Cir. 1990). Judge Noonan wrote a powerful and passionate article on the Harris case that overlaps substantially with this chapter's narrative while examining the moral issues at greater length. Noonan, *Horses of the Night: Harris v. Vasquez*, 45 Stan. L. Rev. 1011 (1993).

Nine months later Robert Harris went on trial in the Superior Court of San Diego County. He was charged with two counts of murder. He retracted his confession. His defense was innocence: he had not shot the boys. He was found guilty.

The jury then entered on "the penalty phase." By statute the jury was directed to "take into account and be guided by the aggravating and mitigating circumstances referred to in this section." These circumstances included the defendant's ability "to conform his conduct to the requirements of the law was impaired as a result of mental disease" and "the circumstances of the crime of which the defendant was convicted in the present proceeding." The statute did not specify what circumstances should be aggravating or what mitigating.

Under this statute the state of California was able to show that in 1975 Harris had beaten a man to death and had been convicted of voluntary manslaughter. The state also showed that while waiting his current trial for murder Harris had presided over a kangaroo court that had convicted another prisoner of "cowardice" and had sentenced him to be forcibly sodomized; Harris had carried out the sentence.

In his own behalf Harris took the stand, repudiated his denial of guilt, and expressed sorrow for the murders. He described "a dismal childhood." His father was twice convicted of incest with his sisters. His mother was convicted of bank robbery. His father had beaten him savagely. His education ended in the seventh grade. In rebuttal Dr. Griswold, the psychiatrist, testified that Harris had an "antisocial personality" and as such was unlikely to restrain himself.

The jury voted for death. On March 6, 1979, the trial judge, having made an independent determination, agreed and imposed the sentence of death. Harris was twenty-six.

No execution had been carried out in California since 1968. At the time Harris's conviction took place there were thirty other prisoners sentenced to death and housed in the section of the prison popularly known as death row. When the state decided to reinvigorate the death penalty, Harris was an obvious choice. He was white, not black; racial animus could not be suspected. He had confessed to the murders before trial and after trial; there was no plausible claim of coercion or mistake. The killings were almost motiveless; the random choice of the victims increased their cruelty. Those he had murdered were innocent children. Who would want to spare his life?

No one, perhaps, for his sake alone; a small number of persons opposed in principle to the death penalty. They numbered in their ranks the brilliant appellate lawyer, Anthony Amsterdam, and the National Association for the Advancement of Colored People, which understood that African Americans were disproportionately subjected to execution. In time these defenders of Harris's life were supplemented by the American Civil Liberties Union challenging the fairness of the sentencing. In popular terms, the struggle was over the death penalty. If it could not be imposed on Harris, on whom could it be imposed?

A colleague of mine on the circuit, Alex Kozinski, once wrote for The New Yorker an article entitled "Confessions of a Death Penalty Judge."[2] It is an acutely sensitive article describing Judge Kozinski's feelings in cases analogous to Harris—cases where a state prisoner, condemned to die by a state judge, has come into the federal system; invoked the classic remedy for constitutional injury, the writ of habeas corpus; and asked the federal courts to set aside his conviction or his punishment because state proceedings violated the federal Constitution. If the prisoner's petition for habeas corpus is successful, the prisoner will receive a new trial or a new sentencing; at least temporarily his life will be prolonged. In that elementary sense, his life or death is at stake in the federal proceeding. But the federal proceeding is not itself a criminal trial. It is styled, in federal speak, a civil action. The federal judges do not pronounce sentence of death. The federal judge only determines if the state criminal proceedings were affected by mistakes as to what the federal Constitution required.

Because of the limited scope of our responsibility and our power, I did not think of myself as a death penalty judge. I was not voting on the death penalty. I was voting on whether Harris had been tried and sentenced as the Constitution, as interpreted by the Supreme Court and our circuit, demanded. I was not engaged in punishing crime or affording clemency but in the familiar exercise of reading and honoring precedent. That the death of Harris turned on the outcome was not my focus. Nonetheless, in my years of involvement with the case, its life or death

---

2. Alex Kozinski (born 1950) was chief judge of the U.S. Claims Court (1982–85) and served on the Ninth Circuit from 1985 until 2017 (chief judge 2007–14). The text refers to his article *Tinkering With Death: A Death-Penalty Judge Reflects: How Does It Feel To Send Another Man To Die?*, New Yorker, Feb. 10, 1997.

character came to color the context in which the case was treated and, ultimately, to affect my understanding of the Supreme Court itself.

My first encounter with the case came in my first year on the court in argument on November 5, 1986 in Pasadena. Presiding was Arthur Alarcón, former pardons secretary of Governor Edmund Brown and former California judge, a man used to assessing the merits of capital cases with a cool eye; he had been President Carter's choice to be the first Hispanic member of our court.[3] Joining him was Melvin Brunetti (once a partner in Reno of Senator Laxalt), appointed to our court by President Reagan; he was a practical-minded man.

At the time Harris's case reached us, he had lost in a mandatory review of the case by the California Supreme Court and certiorari had been denied by the United States Supreme Court.[4] He had twice petitioned unsuccessfully for habeas in the state courts. He had petitioned once before in federal district court for habeas and lost, then won in the Ninth Circuit, then lost in the United States Supreme Court. We were looking at his second federal habeas petition, denied by the district court.

Without much difficulty our panel reached the same result unanimously.[5] We held that San Diego had not been so saturated with stories of the murder that an impartial jury could not have been chosen. We held that his lawyer had not been ineffective in deciding not to introduce an electroencephalogram or EEG done in 1971 reflecting abnormalities, when one done in 1977 showed nothing unusual. We held that it was not contrary to the Constitution for the trial judge to exclude from the jury those who were opposed to the death penalty, thereby producing what was called a "death-qualified" jury. We held that Harris had not made a showing sufficient to entitle him to further discovery, or that California purposely discriminated in executing killers who were men between the age of 25 and 34 whose victims were white. None of his arguments were frivolous. None were winning. The opinion, prepared by Judge Alarcón, was issued almost three years after the oral argument. It reflected a care-

---

3. Arthur L. Alarcón (1925–2015) was a California superior court judge (1964–78), and an associate justice on a California court of appeal (1978–79) before his service on the Ninth Circuit (1979–2015). On Judge Brunetti, see page 84 n. 8.

4. *People v. Harris*, 623 P.2d 240, 243 (Cal.), *cert. denied*, 454 U.S. 882 (1981). The online history of Harris's state and federal proceedings is complex. Citations are provided where they seem useful.

5. *Harris v. Pulley*, 885 F.2d 1354 (9th Cir. 1988).

ful scrutiny of all the lawyerly objections and a meticulous refutation of them. I do not recall being troubled either by the analysis or by the outcome leaving Harris's sentence undisturbed. I do recall communicating to an older colleague, Ted Goodwin, my surprise that nine years had elapsed since Harris had been condemned to die.[6] "Death penalty cases usually take about a dozen years," he replied laconically.

I didn't think about the case for over two years. In the meantime, it traveled once more to the Supreme Court, which denied cert., and once more to the federal district court, which denied a new petition for habeas. The latter decision was appealed to us. At the spring symposium in Santa Barbara, an occasion for the judges of the circuit court to meet informally, Judge Alarcón observed to me that we would be getting the case in April and asked whether, if he and Judge Brunetti were not in San Francisco, I would be willing to handle it alone. I wasn't familiar with any precedent permitting one judge to act for the entire panel, but I replied affirmatively.

In April 1992, the case arrived. It arrived with great fanfare in the media. The logjam in executions in California was to be broken. No chance remained for Harris. The state had set the date when he should die. It was 12:01 A.M., Tuesday morning, April 3.

My two panel colleagues left the case to me. No doubt my agreement with Judge Alarcón's opinion in 1988 had assured them that I would affirm the district court again; they did not, I believe, anticipate that Harris's appeal would amount to anything. In the meantime, particularly due to my son John, I had become more conscious of how the death penalty weighed on the consciences of his generation. The issue now presented by Harris was new. I took a new look.

The issue on the merits was whether Harris at his sentencing had been entitled to the services of a psychiatrist paid for by the state. Constitutional law at the time of the trial acknowledged no such entitlement. Six years later, in 1985, constitutional law had changed. In an 8–1 decision, the Supreme Court held that if the state employed a psychiatrist in a capital case, fundamental fairness required the state to pay for a psy-

---

6. Alfred Theodore Goodwin (1923–2022) was an Oregon circuit court judge (1955–60), a justice on the Oregon Supreme Court (1960–69), and a federal district judge (1969–71), before his appointment to the Ninth Circuit in 1971. After his service as chief judge (1988–91) he took senior status, and at his death he was the oldest active federal judge.

chiatrist chosen by an indigent defendant.[7] Realistically, the Supreme Court assumed that a psychiatrist would testify to help the side which offered his testimony. The jury would decide the battle of experts. The state would not have an extra advantage that the defendant could not afford. If Harris had been tried in 1986, he would have had the benefit of this decision. But was the decision retroactive?

The retroactivity of a constitutional decision by the Supreme Court requires balancing. On the one hand, it may be thought that, if the Supreme Court says this is what the Constitution requires, then the Constitution has always required it. The words of the Constitution haven't changed. If their meaning is clearer now, why shouldn't that meaning be applied to all cases or at least to cases still in the process of appeal? On the other hand, when the Supreme Court discovers a new meaning in the Constitution, it has effectively changed the law. Are all trials that were conducted under the old law to be redone? Even to apply the new law to cases on appeal has the potentiality of unsetting results lawfully reached under the law at the time of trial. How fair is it to ask prosecutors to redo their once-lawful work?

The Supreme Court has resolved the dilemma by laying down three criteria.[8] The new meaning of the Constitution must go to fundamental fairness. It must enhance the accuracy of factfinding. It must be of "watershed" significance. If these criteria were met, the new constitutional law was to be applied retroactively.

I had little doubt that the 1985 decision met these criteria. The decision itself said its requirement was a matter of fundamental fairness. The addition of a second psychiatrist's perspective enhanced the accuracy of factfinding. The new requirement was analogous to the discovery by the Supreme Court in 1963 in *Gideon* that the Constitution assured an indigent defendant in a felony case the right to a state-subsidized lawyer.[9] A psychiatrist was not as essential as counsel, but in a case where life or death might turn on the defendant's mental capacity, the right to a psychiatrist witness was of capital importance. The new rule seemed to me a watershed.

Sitting alone, I did not have to go this far to decide what to do. All I had to decide was whether to postpone Harris's execution long enough

7. *Ake v. Oklahoma*, 470 U.S. 68 (1985).

8. *Teague v. Lane*, 489 U.S. 288 (1989).

9. *Gideon v. Wainwright*, 372 U.S. 335 (1963).

for this issue to be presented to the full panel. Supreme Court precedent on this point was decisive. If "reasonable jurists" could think the merits of an appeal were obvious, or even if reasonable jurists would disagree as to the merits, the stay should be granted so that a decision on the merits could be reached after proper consideration.[10] Death was not to be permitted to cut off the case before the merits of the appeal were decided. I had no doubt at all that reasonable jurists would at least find Harris's contention debatable. Accordingly, I prepared a short opinion stating this conclusion, culminating in an order staying his execution until his arguments were heard by the full panel.

I then left our courthouse at Seventh and Mission and walked to the federal district courthouse at 450 Golden Gate Avenue to hear both sides argue about the stay. It is not unusual for a judge to have made up his mind before oral argument. Oral argument affords him one last chance to check his certainties.

Nothing that was said changed mine. I read my opinion aloud. I avoided the press and photographers lined up on the steps of 450. It was all over in less than an hour. It was Friday, March 31, three days before the date scheduled for the execution.

The state of California was prepared for the setback it received. On Saturday, the state filed its appeal in the United States Supreme Court, seeking the lifting of my stay. On Monday, April 1, the Supreme Court ruled. Six to three the stay was sustained. I wondered to myself how three of the justices could not see that the issue of retroactivity was at a minimum debatable.

Harris's execution did not take place. My decision aroused the towering indignation of the media in San Diego and even of talk shows in San Francisco. Mary Lee, setting out to get groceries, heard me denounced on the car radio as a monster who had already delayed Harris's execution "for a dozen years." She did a U-turn, returned to the house, and called the station to say I hadn't been on the court a dozen years.

Other consequences of the stay were less predictable. Justice Kennedy called the court to say that when he had sat on the case when he was on the circuit in 1984, there had been a danger of violence from persons angry that retribution for Harris had been postponed. This warning was sufficiently sharp that the court administrators asked me if I wanted protection by the marshals. It seemed prudent to say yes.

10. *Barefoot v. Estelle*, 463 U.S. 880, 893–94 (1983).

Marshals duly arrived. They followed me home in their own car. They took up a position in the driveway and elsewhere outside the house. They refused our offer of coffee. They were on duty. Their vigilance induced in us a sense of danger.

On Monday, I went to work. The marshals left Mary Lee unprotected. A friend, Gretchen Ward, the sister of Attorney General John Van der Kamp, telephoned and mentioned the hazards run by her brother. As they talked, Mary Lee notice a strange woman crouching in our backyard, a good thirty yards from the street. "May I help you," Mary Lee called out. The woman said she was looking for her dog and was later seen on the street with him. The momentary menace passed.

The marshals, accompanying me to lunch, did not join me to eat. Walking to the restaurant together, their leader discoursed on the behaviors of "mopes," adding to the range of references in my vocabulary for habitual criminals. The next day was a teaching day for me at Boalt in my course on Professional Responsibility. I gave out assignments for oral reports to be made the next week. At the end of the session a young man I had assigned a topic came up to me. "I'm one of the marshals," he said, offering a clarification but not seeking an excuse. I told him not to feel obliged.

By Friday, we had had enough of the claustrophobia induced by being guarded. We accepted an invitation from old friends, Harry and Anne Newman, to spend the weekend with them in Indian Wells. I decided that the imagined assailants would never track us there. We said goodbye to the marshals at the airport.

In May, the panel heard argument on the merits of Harris's contention. I took the lead in questioning the state's response. Judge Alarcón called a recess and in chambers told me he would not sit on the bench if I continued my questions. I said I thought my questions were entirely appropriate. Judge Brunetti seemed undecided but then remained with Judge Alarcón while I returned to the bench alone. I let my colleagues know when my questions were over, and they came back. I had never experienced such a situation before and have never experienced such a one since.

Eventually, 2–1, the panel voted to reject Harris's appeal based on the absence of a psychiatrist speaking as his witness. The panel dryly quoted the American Psychiatric Association on "the evolving and inexact nature of the psychiatric discipline" and held that a debate between psychiatrists would not enhance the accuracy of factfinding by the jury.[11] Surprisingly enough, however, the panel majority found possible merit in another claim that had struck me as worthy of little consideration. It was that Harris had been set up by the state planting an informer in his cell. The panel remanded for the district court to take evidence on this point. The march to execution was derailed.

It took two years for the case to return to us. In this, his fourth habeas petition, Harris appealed the district court's finding that his informer claim was baseless and that other issues had as little weight. This fourth habeas petition was unanimously denied, but on request of a colleague, a stay of execution was granted pending an en banc vote. This stay served ultimately to confuse the Supreme Court. Meanwhile, Harris's execution was again scheduled, this time for 12:01 A.M., Tuesday, April 21, 1992, two days after Easter.

On Good Friday, April 17, a class action was begun by the American Civil Liberties Union in the federal court in San Francisco. The ACLU sought to enjoin all executions in California on the grounds that death by lethal gas was cruel and unusual punishment. If the ACLU was right, Harris's execution would have to be stopped. Judge Marilyn Patel[12] heard argument on Saturday and decided that the ACLU's contention required briefing by both sides. She set a date a month later for the briefs to be filed. Pending her decision, she stayed the execution.

The state of California was again prepared to cope with a setback. The state immediately filed an appeal with us, asking for a writ of mandamus dissolving Judge Patel's stay. Judge Alarcón scheduled oral argument for the afternoon of Easter Sunday. Early in the evening of that day, the panel voted, 2–1, to issue the writ requested by the state.[13]

Mandamus is a special sort of remedy, a command issued to the district court. It is relatively rare. The appeals court cannot simply snap its fingers and say, Obey. It is bound to issue a reasoned opinion. For whatever reason, there was a considerable delay before the panel majority produced their opinion. When it was transmitted to the court, the time was Monday, about 3:00 P.M. The execution was nine hours and one minute away.

---

11. *Harris v. Vasquez*, 949 F.2d 1497, 1521 n. 21 (9th Cir. 1990)

12. Marilyn Hall Patel (born 1938) was a district judge from 1980 to 2012 (chief judge 1997–2004).

13. *Gomez v. U.S. Dist. Ct. for N. Dist. of California*, 966 F.2d 460 (9th Cir. 1992).

Under our existing rules, when a panel decided a death penalty case, a stay of its order came into force if a judge asked for it in order to allow the full court to take the case en banc if it wished. As our panel had assumed jurisdiction of the appeal as the panel assigned to Harris's death penalty case, I assumed a stay would be granted upon request. Two judges made the request. The panel, 2–1, declined to grant it. In the view of the majority, the suit brought in San Francisco was not a death penalty suit. The death penalty rules did not apply.

Judge William Norris and I were unsatisfied by this response.[14] The panel had taken the appeal because it was the Harris panel. How could its decision not be a death penalty decision? We put this question to the Chief Judge, Clifford Wallace, but he did not think that he had authority to overrule the panel. That could only be done by an en banc vote.

The judges of the circuit were scattered up and down the West Coast, but one was on duty in Guam and another was visiting a daughter in Massachusetts. None were expecting to be called after work. By the time we had a full sense of the situation it was evening. Our headquarters was in transition. Forced out of our courthouse by the Loma Prieta earthquake, we had temporary offices on Market Street in the process of transfer to Spear Street. There the central staff and in particular the indomitable Jeri Curtis, who maintained our contact with San Quentin, were at work. At 6:00 P.M., my law clerks and I moved to Spear Street. Jim Shannon, one of my clerks, talked to a friend clerking at the Supreme Court. "The blood lust is high tonight," Jim was informed.

I and other judges who agreed with me that the mandamus action was subject to the death penalty rules started calling our colleagues. By 10:00 P.M., ten judges had agreed that the rule on death penalty stays should apply. Jeri Curtis called the warden at San Quentin to stop the execution.

Meanwhile, the stay requested on the fragile fourth habeas petition was still in effect. The state of California had petitioned the Supreme Court to dissolve it. The Supreme Court did so at 11:30 P.M., Pacific Coast Time, 2:30 A.M. in Washington, D.C. The timing was such that the Supreme Court obviously anticipated there would be no more stays once the fourth habeas petition had been eliminated.

But the ten-judge stay had intervened. Moreover, at 11:45 P.M. (PDT), just after the Supreme Court had acted, and seemingly in response to it,

14. William A. Norris (1927–2017) was a Ninth Circuit judge (1980–97).

another stay was entered, the third of that day. This stay came about by a poll taken by the Chief Judge on whether the Harris panel should recognize that its mandamus action fell under the death penalty rules for stays. By 11:00 P.M., a majority of the court had so voted. The chief judge notified the panel. The panel acquiesced. At 11:45 P.M., this new, third stay was entered by the Ninth Circuit. It was not a retort to the Supreme Court. It was a rectification of a position taken by its own members. Failure to know what was going on led to Robert Bork's later misinterpretation of this scenario as rebellious.[15]

At midnight, both the second and third stays were in effect. Harris's execution was postponed. The judges of the Harris panel left their post. I drove home to Berkeley. But the Supreme Court of the United States—it was now 3:00 A.M. in Washington—did not sleep nor slumber.

By telephone (it could not have been by a collegial gathering of the justices in one room, it is unknown if it was by conference call) the Supreme Court voted 7–2, to dissolve the second and third stays.[16] The State of California was free to execute Harris. The word reached the warden at San Quentin at about 3:30 A.M. (PDT).

Harris was escorted into the gas chamber. His lawyer, Michael Laurence, made two more efforts. He called me at home and told me what the Supreme Court had done and asked me for a new stay. I said, "I can't do any more." Laurence then called Judge Harry Pregerson, notable both for courage and magnanimity, who issued a new stay of execution at about 5:30 A.M. (PDT). Harris was removed from the chamber. At 6:00 A.M., the Supreme Court replied. Time was now extraordinarily compressed. Justice Blackmun, who had dissented from the earlier order, was not consulted. The Court dissolved Judge Pregerson's writ and commanded that no further stays be issued without the Supreme Court's approval. The order was effective and final. Harris was put to death at 6:30 in the morning, our time.

Among the sequellae to this night were these events: On April 27, 1992, I published an op-ed piece in the New York Times criticizing the Supreme Court's action. I borrowed from Chief Justice John Marshall an

---

15. Robert H. Bork, *An Outbreak of Judicial Civil Disobedience,* Wall St. J., Apr. 29, 1992, at A19. Bork (1927–2012) served on the D.C. Circuit (1982–88). In 1987, he was nominated to be an associate justice on the Supreme Court, but he was not confirmed by the Senate.

16. *Vasquez v. Harris,* 503 U.S. 1000 (1992).

expression for severe disagreement with a constitutional decision: it was "treason to the constitution."[17] My position elicited two strong rebuttals and more than a dozen letters of agreement from other federal judges around the country.

On May 6, as I contemplated an answer to one of my critics, I suffered a heart attack. The physical conditions leading to it preexisted Harris. The emotions aroused by the last three days of the case could be seen as the precipitating cause.

On October 4, 1994, Judge Patel ruled on the class action suit directed against death by lethal gas. Noting that only three states still retained this method; that one of them, Maryland, had executed no one since 1962; that a second, Arizona, was in the process of changing the law; and that only California was actually using gas, Judge Patel ruled it cruel and unusual. On February 21, 1996, the Ninth Circuit affirmed her decision. The state of California did not appeal.[18] Robert Alton Harris had been put to death in a way that in hindsight violated the Constitution.[19]

---

17. *Cohens v. Virginia*, 19 U.S. (6 Wheat.) 264, 404 (1821). For the text of Judge Noonan's op-ed, see Appendix F.

18. *Fierro v. Gomez*, 865 F. Supp. 1387, 1388 (N.D. Cal. 1994), *aff'd*, 77 F.3d 301 (9th Cir. 1996). The state did in fact petition successfully for cert. The Supreme Court vacated the Ninth Circuit's decision for reconsideration in light of an amendment to the state death penalty statute that allowed the prisoner to choose between lethal gas and lethal injection as the means of execution and made lethal injection the default method. *Gomez v. Fierro*, 519 U.S. 918 (1996). On remand, a Ninth Circuit panel declined to reach the merits on lack of standing and ripeness grounds, and instructed the district court to vacate its previous decision. *Fierro v. Terhune*, 147 F.3d 1158 (9th Cir. 1998). Judge Pregerson dissented: "Both the district court and this court found that execution by gas is cruel and unusual punishment. By refusing to address the merits of this case, we are compounding the cruelty by precluding a condemned individual from challenging the legality of his punishment unless he first chooses an unconstitutional method of execution. This is a cruel hoax." *Id.* at 1160.

19. Judge Noonan's conclusion about Harris's death correctly states the law of the Constitution, at least in the view of the Ninth Circuit. In *LaGrand v. Stewart*, 173 F.3d 1144 (9th Cir. 1999), a panel consisting of Chief Judge Hug and Judges Pregerson and T.G. Nelson held that Arizona's method of using lethal gas, which the state conceded was "substantially similar" to California's, violated the Eighth Amendment. In doing so, Judge Nelson's opinion for the unanimous court quoted Judge Patel's factual findings in *Gomez*, and pointed out that "no court has ever said the district court was wrong"; Nelson treated the Ninth Circuit merits decision in *Gomez* as clearly correct and controlling. *Id.* at 1148–49. Subsequent decisions cite the merits analysis in *Gomez* as authoritative. *See, e.g.*, *Wood v. Ryan*, 759 F.3d 1076, 1087 (9th Cir. 2014).

THIRTEEN

# Three Strikes and Not Out[1]

ISAAC RAMIREZ, IN COMPANY WITH HIS SISTER, shoplifted merchandise from a Lucky's grocery store. They left the store in a car, driven by a third person, which hit the foot of a security guard causing a minor injury to him. Nine months later, Ramirez committed shoplifting at a K-Mart; as he ran out of the store, he pushed a security guard with his open hand. Shortly afterwards, he was apprehended and charged with both crimes. As in each case force had been used on a security guard, each case was charged as robbery, a felony. Ramirez was told that his sister was in serious trouble if he did not plead guilty. He accepted a plea bargain: to plead guilty to the two felonies and be sentenced to one year in county jail. He was released after six months.

These events occurred in 1991 in Orange County, California. Five years later, in May 1996, Ramirez was caught walking out of a Sears department store carrying a VCR, which he had wrapped in security tape and not paid for. The VCR was priced at $199. The crime itself was petty theft. When connected to his previous convictions, the theft became "a wobbler," that is, it could be treated either as a misdemeanor or as a felony. The prosecutor had discretion as to how it would be charged. The prosecutor charged it as a felony, thereby invoking the provisions of California's Three Strikes Law, enacted in 1994. Under that law, the trial judge had discretion not to count the earlier convictions as strikes. He declined to exercise this discretion. The judge noted that Ramirez had brought into the store the tape that secured the VCR and had a customer

1. *Ramirez v. Castro*, 365 F.3d 755, 756 (9th Cir. 2004).

in mind to whom to sell it, proof, the judge said, of sophistication and planning: "What's happened is that Mr. Ramirez has become a professional thief, and it's just real clear from all the evidence." Ramirez stated that the sentence would fall on his children. The judge: "But I'm not the one doing that. I'm afraid that you're the one who did that when you committed the offense." Applying the Three Strikes Law, the judge sentenced Ramirez to state prison for twenty-five years to life.

Ramirez appealed his conviction as cruel and unusual, in violation of the constitutions of California and the United States. The state Court of Appeal held the punishment not disproportionate to his recidivism. Ramirez had failed to "take advantage of" two attempts by the state to rehabilitate him. The court did not note that "the two attempts" consisted only in the single six months in county jail. This court's pronouncement was the last word on the subject from the state judicial system.[2] The Supreme Court of California summarily denied review. His state petition for habeas corpus was denied by both the California Court of Appeal and the California Supreme Court.

It was not a ground of appeal that Ramirez's punishment was the result of two discretionary calls—the call of the prosecutor that turned the shoplifting wobbler into a felony; the call of the trial judge to count the earlier convictions as strikes. We boast at times that we are a government of laws, not men. Here, the most important feature of the case, the sentence, was determined not by law but by the choices made by the prosecutor and the trial judge.

In May 2000, after three years' incarceration in Ironwood State Prison, a Security Level III facility for inmates with "several prior prison terms or significant behavioral problems," Ramirez turned to the federal courts. The district court in Los Angeles assigned his case to Magistrate Judge Andrew Wistrich.[3] While the case awaited decision, a majority of a panel of our court composed of Chief Judge Mary Schroeder and Judge Richard Paez[4] held that application of Three Strikes Law in another case involving theft from a K-Mart, *Andrade*, did constitute cruel

---

2. The court of appeal's unpublished opinion is quoted in *id.* at 760.

3. Andrew J. Wistrich (born 1950) was a federal magistrate judge (1994–2018).

4. Mary Murphy Schroeder (born 1940) was appointed to the Ninth Circuit in 1979 and served as chief judge (2000–2007). Richard A. Paez (born 1947) was a district judge (1994–2000) before taking a seat on the Ninth Circuit in 2000.

and unusual punishment.[5] Encouraged by this precedent, the magistrate judge recommended the same result for Ramirez. J. Spencer Letts, a careful and conscientious district judge, accepted the recommendation and granted habeas.[6] Ramirez, by now a prisoner of the state for five years, became a free man. The state appealed.

As the appeal traveled to us, *Andrade* reached the United States Supreme Court.[7] In an opinion by Sandra O'Connor the court found Andrade's sentences of twenty-five years to life not grossly disproportionate to his crimes. Andrade had begun committing burglaries in 1982 and in 1983 had been sentenced to ten years imprisonment. Released early, he was convicted in 1988 of transporting marijuana and sentenced to eight years in federal prison. He later received another federal sentence of six years for transporting marijuana. He was, besides, a heroin addict. His K-Mart thefts were at the end of a string of crimes. The principle governing what was cruel and unusual was proportionality. The "precise contours" of the principle, Justice O'Connor wrote, were not established. The state court's sentence in *Andrade* was not an unreasonable application of the Supreme Court's reading of the Eighth Amendment. With its victory in *Andrade*, the state of California thought its appeal in *Ramirez* must succeed.

We heard the appeal in Pasadena on July 28, 2003. The "we" consisted of Andy Kleinfeld, and Kim Wardlaw and me. Judge Kleinfeld has already appeared in this narrative as a judge deeply committed to the requirements of the law. Judge Wardlaw, after serving as a federal district court judge, had joined our court in 1998, enhancing it with her energy, penetrating insights, and, above all, by her indomitable spirit.[8] The panel was a pleasure for me to be with.

Isaac Ramirez argued his own case. A deputy attorney general from San Diego appeared for the state in its unusual posture of appellant. She told the court immediately that *Andrade* was dispositive because, as the Supreme Court had declared, the contours of the proportionality prin-

5. *Andrade v. Att'y Gen. of California*, 270 F.3d 743 (9th Cir. 2001).

6. John Spencer Letts (1934–2014) was a district judge from 1985 until his death.

7. *Lockyer v. Andrade*, 538 U.S. 63 (2003).

8. Kim McLane Wardlaw (born 1954) was a district judge 1995 before her appointment to the Ninth Circuit.

ciple were unclear;[9] the state court could not have acted unreasonably in finding proportionality in the sentences of Ramirez.

I asked how we should go about determining what was gross disproportionality. There followed this dialogue:

Deputy Attorney General: "Well, your honor, unfortunately, the U.S. Supreme Court has indicated that the application and the contours of that principle are not clear. And the U.S. Supreme Court, I believe, has really not made that clear. So in terms of the actual principle itself the US. Supreme Court did say that it is up to the legislature, the state legislatures to determine, it's within the legislatures' discretion in terms of how to interpret that gross disproportionality."

The Court [Noonan]: "Hasn't the state of California done that by making much less penalties for much more serious crimes? Do you know what the penalty for rape is?"

Deputy Attorney General: "I don't know the exact penalties right off hand, your honor, I don't."

I had learned that Stephen Cooley, the district attorney for Los Angeles county, had campaigned for office on the platform that he would not automatically seek application of the Three Strikes Law. After election in 2000, he had issued this policy directive to his deputies:

> The Three Strikes law, Penal Code Section Section 1170.12(a)-(d), provides a powerful tool for obtaining life sentences in cases involving habitual criminal offenders. However, unless used judiciously, it also has the potential for injustice and abuse in the form of disproportionately harsh sentences for relatively minor crimes. The Three Strikes statutory scheme appropriately authorizes the use of prosecutorial discretion in its implementation. As prosecutors, it is our legal and ethical obligation to exercise this discretion in a manner that assures proportionality, evenhanded application, predictability and consistency. Moreover, the potential for coercive plea-bargaining must be avoided. Penal Code Section 1170.12(d)(2) authorizes prosecutors to move to dismiss or strike a qualifying prior felony conviction in the furtherance of justice pursuant to Penal Code Section 1885. In this context, "in furtherance of justice" requires consideration of the constitutional rights of the defendant and the interests of society. [citations] Proper exercise of prosecutorial discretion protects society and preserves confidence in a respect for the criminal justice system.

9. The clause seems to be missing a word, so I have inserted "principle."

I was curious, with this approach taken by the prosecutor in the largest California county, why the state was so rigid in the case of Ramirez. The deputy attorney general said that she didn't live in Los Angeles and knew nothing of the policy set by its prosecutor. Judge Wardlaw, after stating what she knew the Los Angeles policy to be, added: "So now what I'm asking you since you're a representative of our state and maybe you might want to take this back to Mr. Lockyer.[10] I'm asking you, What is the state's interest in putting this man back in prison for life when you're going to have to pay the jail cost and all of that and this man, you have a record that he's been out of prison now for what, for over a year and there's been no shoplifting, no evidence of any crime. He's got all these letters saying what a great citizen he is. Why does the state want to take this man and put him in jail? I don't understand what Mr. Lockyer's interest is in that."

Deputy Attorney General: "Well, your honor, if I may. Hopefully I can answer all of your questions. Mr. Lockyer's interest is in upholding the laws of the state of California. The laws of the state of California as determined by the California legislature and by the people of the state of California by ballot initiative has been to punish recidivists more severely."

Judge Kleinfeld intervened: "When I was in practice I used to get really bothered by sentencing policies sometimes because it seemed like when I did criminal defense my clients didn't get punished much for hurting people but they got severely punished if they offended the court by doing what they promised the court they wouldn't do again. And that was really the motivation for the harshness toward recidivism. It was the probation officer felt like he had been goaded if he had given my client a break and then my client reoffended. It was more like offending the court was a bigger deal than hurting somebody. That's wrong. Just flat morally wrong. And you know, none of us are immune from that kind of concern. However, I have a real hard time distinguishing this case from *Andrade* where the guy just shoplifted 150 bucks worth of video tapes. And I'm wondering is there any value in this case to deferring submission and giving you a chance to talk with opposing counsel or are you just like the lawyer in the last case. No authority, a waste of time."

Deputy Attorney General: "Well, your honor, I believe that the authority is under *Lockyer v. Andrade*."

---

10. William W. Lockyer was attorney general of California (1999–2007).

Judge Kleinfeld: "You don't understand what I said. When I say authority I mean authority to negotiate as opposed to legal authority which we must follow as precedent. You might have noticed that you didn't have to argue to me that *Andrade* was good authority for your position because I just said to you *Andrade* was good authority for your position."

Deputy Attorney General: "Well your honor, I don't believe, hope that I can answer your question. I don't believe that I have authority to enter into discussions with opposing counsel."

Judge Wardlaw: "I'd like to ask you to go back to Mr. Lockyer and tell him that I asked you to do it and tell him, ask him whether he would give you some authority to negotiate this case based on Mr. Ramirez's conduct since being released from prison. Have you done that yet?"

When the argument was finished, Isaac Ramirez rejoined his pastor and the supporters from his evangelical church. They were weeping, and he cried with them at the back of the courtroom.

Kim Wardlaw wrote the opinion affirming the order of habeas. Ramirez's sentence, we held, was grossly disproportionate to his crime of shoplifting, even when that crime was considered as his third criminal offense. He had received the highest sentence possible in California, save only death or imprisonment for life. Neither murder in the second degree nor manslaughter nor rape would have required such a sentence. No other state in the nation had a statute that would have authorized the punishment meted out to Ramirez for the offenses he had committed. The four states whose sentencing laws came closest—Louisiana, Rhode Island, Texas, and West Virginia—all had provisions which would have made the result in Ramirez's case unlikely or impossible. If Ramirez had committed his crimes in a place under federal jurisdiction and had been convicted of them by the United States, he would have been sentenced to one to seven months. By all these objective criteria—the criminal law of California, the criminal laws of the 49 other states, the federal Sentencing Guidelines—the sentence imposed on Ramirez bore no fair relation to what he had done. It was grossly disproportionate.

That conclusion was not the end of Wardlaw's opinion but the necessary first step. Under the terms of AEDPA, a federal court could only override the judgment of a state court on a question of constitutional law if the state court had applied a Supreme Court decision "unreasonably."[11] It was not enough, the Supreme Court had said, upping the re-

11. "AEDPA" is the Antiterrorism and Effective Death Act of 1996.

quirements of AEDPA, that the state court had made a mistake.[12] The mistake had to be an unreasonable mistake. A judge, the Supreme Court thought, could be in error but reasonably in error. Unreasonableness had to be found if habeas was to be granted.[13]

It was unreasonable, Judge Wardlaw went on, for the state court to say that Ramirez had had two earlier chances at rehabilitation when in fact he'd been sentenced to jail only once before. It was unreasonable for the state court not to note the nonviolent nature of Ramirez's three strikes, his minimal criminal history, and his only prior sentence of six months in a county jail. Objectively unreasonable, the decision of the California Court of Appeal had violated the Eighth Amendment to the Constitu-

12. *Williams v. Taylor*, 529 U.S. 362, 410 (2000).

13. *See also Bradley v. Henry*, 428 F.3d 811, 816 (9th Cir. 2005) (Noonan, Cir. J., for the court):

> Habeas corpus is a fundamental right secured by the Constitution of the United States. U.S. Const. art. I., § 9, cl. 2. Its exercise is presently governed by the Antiterrorism and Effective Death Penalty Act (AEDPA), 28 U.S.C. § 2254(d)(1). As governed by this statute, the great writ may be issued only if the state court's ruling "resulted in a decision that was contrary to, or involved an unreasonable application of, clearly established Federal law, as determined by the Supreme Court of the United States" or was "based on an unreasonable determination of the facts in light of the evidence presented in the State court proceeding." *Id.*
>
> It is not difficult to determine when a decision is contrary to federal law established by the Supreme Court: it is a decision reaching a different result from the result reached by the Supreme Court on "facts that are materially indistinguishable ...." *See Williams v. Taylor*, 529 U.S. 362, 406 (2000). It is more difficult to determine whether a state court's ruling "involved an unreasonable application" of controlling precedent from the Supreme Court. Nearly every case is different. The statutory term "unreasonable" invites debate as to what is or is not reasonable. "Applying a general standard to a specific case can demand a substantial element of judgment." *See Yarborough v. Alvarado*, 541 U.S. 652, 664 (2004). We are admonished that the test is not our view of what would be erroneous but what is "objectively unreasonable." *See Lockyer v. Andrade*, 538 U.S. 63, 76 (2003).
>
> No doubt there is an insidious implication in this admonishment that there is an entirely objective perspective on each case, whereas as we know: "We may try to see things as objectively as we please. None the less, we can never see them with any eyes except our own." Benjamin N. Cardozo, *The Nature of the Judicial Process* 13 (1921). We heed the Supreme Court's advice by attempting with our own subjective abilities to state what we think some hypothetical reasonable jurist would find to be the case.

tion as interpreted by binding precedent of the United States Supreme Court. Ramirez was entitled to his freedom.

Judge Kleinfeld dissented—dissented "respectfully and regretfully." The first adverb often accompanied a dissent; the second was unusual. It candidly expressed a tension in the judge's mind between what he felt was wrong in Ramirez's sentence and what he thought AEDPA required him to do. In the judge's words, Ramirez's sentence was "inappropriately harsh." Hammurabi "limited the penalty to an eye for an eye." The implicit suggestion was that in abandoning this kind of even reciprocity, California was more cruel than an ancient Babylonian king.

Judge Kleinfeld went on to enumerate the problems with an "excessively harsh sentence." It did not serve the purpose of reaffirming social norms. It provided a potential incentive for violent crime by a person facing the third strike maximum. A "reasonable victim" of Ramirez's crimes would not want to visit such vengeance on him. A reasonable person would not "favor spending hundreds of thousands of dollars to incarcerate Ramirez for decades to protect stores from the occasional $200 shoplifting."

Judge Kleinfeld then noted the impression that Ramirez had made upon him in arguing his own case. "He did it so well that I did not realize until well into his argument that he was the petitioner and not the lawyer for the petitioner." The judge's impression based on the record and on his extensive colloquy with him from the bench was that he is "a good and intelligent man whose self-control occasionally gives way." He had already served enough time for any social purpose to be served by punishment.

"But these are all thoughts," Judge Kleinfeld continued, "I would have if I were the sentencing judge. I am not." He—we—had to decide whether upholding the sentence was an unreasonable application of Supreme Court precedent. The verbal formulas used by the Supreme Court were "largely indeterminate." To reach the result that Judge Wardlaw had reached was the work of "subtle parsing" of the precedents. Parsing of this sort was not compatible with the deference owed the state court. We were "not supposed to cut so finely."

The judge concluded: "I would very much like to join the majority." He could not agree that the state court that applied the precedents unreasonably. The sentence was "not just as between California and

Ramirez," but it was "lawful as between the state and federal jurisdictions." The judge lacked the authority to change the sentence.

Rarely have I known a dissent so straightforward in its presentation of the conflict in the dissenter's mind, a dissent so fair to the majority, a dissent that even in its reluctant conclusion underscored the cruelty of the California decision the judge found he had no authority to set aside. It was a dissent as powerful and as eloquent as our majority opinion, and, much as I did not agree with its conclusion, I admired the courage with which Judge Kleinfeld spoke and the sense of his obligation to the law that drove him to dissent.

Ramirez remained at liberty. We waited for the next move by the attorney general of California. We assumed it would be to seek cert. The whole appeal had been argued to us on the assumption that *Andrade* made the case a slam dunk for the state. Would not the attorney general think that he could secure our summary reversal, a citation to *Andrade* doing the job?

No next move came. The attorney general did not seek a rehearing or en banc review or cert. Judge Wardlaw's opinion was the last word.

*Ramirez* was the first time that application of the California Three Strikes Law by a California court had been successfully restrained by a federal court upholding the overarching principles of the Constitution of the United States. Twelve years before, my efforts in *Harris* to achieve an analogous result had been misunderstood by the Supreme Court and undermined. Here the Constitution had been vindicated. In the words of the Hebrew psalmist:[14]

> A man may go out weeping;
> carrying his bag of seeds;
> but he will come back with songs of joy,
> carrying home his sheaves.

14. Psalm 126:6.

FOURTEEN

# The Imaginary Stash House[1]

EXCERPTS FROM
*United States v. Black*,
733 F.3d 294, 313–14, 318
(9th Cir. 2013)

NOONAN, Circuit Judge, dissenting:

"Lead us not into temptation" is part of a prayer familiar to many. But few, I believe, would think of this prayer as addressed to the government of the United States or would think it necessary to address the government with such a request. The present case creates a precedent and sets a framework in which such a prayer addressed to the government becomes comprehensible and probable. Today our court gives our approval to the government tempting persons in the population at large currently engaged in innocent activity and leading them into the commission of a serious crime, which the government will then prosecute.

The government of the United States paid a confidential informant (CI) $100 a day to recruit random persons willing to rob a cocaine stash house. Brought from Miami to Phoenix by Agent Richard Zayas of the Bureau of Alcohol, Tobacco, Firearms, and Explosives (ATF), the CI tes-

1. As mentioned in the Introduction, Judge Noonan apparently intended at one point to write a final chapter titled "The Imaginary Stash House," but if he did, the manuscript is lost. Noonan wrote strong dissents in two cases involving the government's use of a fictitious "stash house": *United States v. Black* and *United States v. Pedrin*. This chapter includes edited versions of Judge Noonan's opinions in both *Black* and *Pedrin* as well as the discussion of the facts in the majority opinion in *Pedrin*.

tified that he went to bars in "a bad part of town" and that he was not instructed to look for particular individuals who were already involved in an ongoing criminal operation, but simply to recruit anyone who showed an interest in his conversation.

The CI described his modus operandi in these words:

> Q All right. And in your efforts to recruit these robbers, what instructions, what specific instructions were you given by Agent Zayas?
>
> A What instructions? Just to go out and, you know, say—just trying to see what I can meet back—you know, meet people. Meet people, see if they know bad guys, you know.
>
> Q Anyone off the street. Is that basically it?
>
> A Pretty much. No, not—yeah. I mean, yeah, I go to the bars.
>
> Q Right. Now, how do you determine if a person is a bad person without knowing them or without observing them being engaged in a crime?
>
> A Well, it's hard to determine. …
>
> Q Does [Agent Zayas] tell you [to] look only for persons who you know are about to commit a crime?
>
> A No.
>
> Q No. And, in fact, you have approached people at restaurants randomly and have raised potential criminal activity, have you not?
>
> A Yes.

The CI selected a seedy bar as a fit place to troll and then trolled for potential defendants. After several tries, the CI was introduced to Simpson, who expressed an interest. The CI brought Simpson to Zayas, who himself was undercover, posing as a former courier of a Mexican drug ring anxious to be revenged on his former associates. Zayas told Simpson of a stash house where once a month there was cocaine awaiting transportation. In a second meeting with Zayas twelve days later, Simpson introduced Black as a recruit to the robbery, adding that no more men would be needed. Zayas suggested Simpson would need more help, and the others agreed to one more. At a third meeting with

Zayas, Simpson, and Black, three more persons were recruited. The next day, Timmons appeared for the first time as the driver. Simpson did not show up, afraid that he was under surveillance. Zayas told the men that he had rented a warehouse to store his portion of the cocaine and asked them to follow him there. Upon reaching the warehouse, the men were arrested by federal agents. Simpson was arrested three months later.

These facts are not disputed. They establish that Zayas and the CI, acting for the ATF, recruited Simpson to rob the stash house and that Zayas encouraged Simpson to increase the number of robbers; that all of the defendants were informed of the plan to rob a stash house; that unknown to them, the stash house itself did not exist; and that Zayas proposed its robbery as the purpose of the plan. From the start when the CI contacted Simpson to the end when Zayas told the crew to follow him to the warehouse, the agents of the government wrote the crime-script and conducted the defendants in the execution of it.

The opinion of the majority does not hesitate to say, "Moreover, the stash house robbery was entirely the ATF's creation, and it was Zayas who set the parameters for how it had to be carried out." Op. at 305. The crimes of conviction, the opinion states, "resulted from an operation created and staged by ATF.... Zayas invented the scenario, including the need for weapons and for a crew, and the amount of cocaine involved." *Id.* at 303. As the majority acknowledges, the government had no particular information about the defendants that would have made them plausible targets of an investigation. There was a "risk inherent," the majority agrees, "that the government could create a criminal enterprise that would not have come into being but for the temptation of a big payday, a work of fiction spun out by government agents to persons vulnerable to such a ploy who would not otherwise have thought of doing such a robbery." *Id.* at 303.

The majority opinion does not give full weight to Zayas's suggesting an increase in the numbers of the conspirators nor to Zayas's directing the conspirators to the location of the imaginary stash house. These omissions apart, the majority opinion lays out in convincing detail how, from beginning to end, the government wrote the script, found those who would act in it, and brought its dupes together so that they could be arrested....

To sum up, use of an imaginary stash house has no effect on the actual circulation of illegal drugs but may make actual stash houses more secure; the imaginary stash house also gives the government essentially unchecked power to increase the number of persons drawn in as robbers by supplying the number of imaginary guards for the drugs and by supplying the amount of imaginary drugs that are supposed to be present. The power exercised by the government is not only to orchestrate the crime but to control and expand those guilty of it. I do not see how this power can be rationally exercised. No standard exists to determine the limits of the government's discretion.

The four defendants were a portion of the population of Phoenix unknown by the government to harbor any specific criminal plans. Never in their past had they been convicted of a crime of such proportions or a federal crime of any kind. They were inveigled by the ATF to agree to commit a crime which in fact was impossible to commit because the stash house they agreed to rob did not exist. Besides providing this imaginary target for their crime, the ATF brought the CI from Miami to recruit them, fed them Zayas's cover story as to his own motivation, told them of the target to be robbed with detail as to its contents and guards, coached them as to the number of persons needed for the job, and directed them to where they would be arrested. The ATF wrote the script, cast the defendants as the actors, and directed the action to its denouement.

The United States has enormous resources that could be used to tempt and trap criminals. If these resources are deployed to bring an ongoing criminal enterprise to justice, the country is well served. If these resources are deployed to fire the imaginations of dreamers of easy wealth and turn them to conspiring to commit a crime, our government has been the oppressor of its people.

Massively involved in the manufacture of the crime, the ATF's actions constitute conduct disgraceful to the federal government. It is not a function of our government to entice into criminal activity unsuspecting people engaged in lawful conduct; not a function to invent a fiction in order to bait a trap for the innocent; not a function to collect conspirators to carry out a script written by the government. As the executive branch of our government has failed to disavow this conduct, it becomes the duty of the judicial branch to refuse to accept these actions as legitimate elements of a criminal case in a federal court.

EXCERPTS FROM
*United States v. Pedrin*
797 F.3d 792
(9th Cir. 2015)

W. FLETCHER, Circuit Judge:

....The defendant in this case, Alex Pedrin, Jr., was the target of a stash-house sting in Arizona in August 2009. The sting was planned by ATF agent Richard Zayas, at the time a 20-year veteran of the bureau.... Zayas met Pedrin through a confidential informant, Jesus Contreras. Contreras was working with Zayas in the ATF's Tucson office. Contreras told Zayas that his nephew, Omar Perez, had called him to "ask[ ] for work," which Contreras understood to mean work stealing drugs. Contreras set up a meeting between Zayas, Perez, and Pedrin on August 17, 2009. The meeting took place in Zayas's car. During a video-recorded conversation in the car, Zayas described himself to Perez and Pedrin as a disgruntled cocaine courier. He told the two men that he knew about a local stash house, guarded by two armed men, that contained between 40 and 50 kilograms of cocaine. Zayas said he was looking for "someone to go in there and take everything." He asked the men, "What do you think?... Can that be done?" Each man assented.

Zayas met with Perez and Pedrin again on August 19. The men agreed that the robbery would take place two days later, on August 21. Zayas pressed Perez and Pedrin for details about their plan. Pedrin responded, "We'll just... go right when you go in so we're all together, you know what I mean?... Put everybody down. Make them tell us where everything is at and then we leave and then we go split it up." In response to Zayas's questions, Pedrin said he and Perez had recruited three other men. Two of them would go into the house with Pedrin and the other would stay outside with Perez. Pedrin told Zayas that he had obtained "walkie talkies and scanners" to facilitate the operation. The details were planned by the defendants themselves. At no point did Zayas instruct Pedrin and Perez how to carry out the robbery.

On August 21, the day of the planned robbery, Zayas met with all five men. Zayas stated again that the stash house contained between 40 and 50 kilograms of cocaine and that it was guarded by at least two armed men. Zayas then instructed Pedrin and the others to follow him to a storage locker at which they were to drop Zayas's share of cocaine after the robbery. On the way to the locker, however, the men became suspicious and pulled into a nearby trailer park. One of the men took a different car to the storage locker location, where he saw ATF agents. He called the others and warned them that it was a sting. The men fled but were picked up by federal and state officers shortly afterward....

NOONAN, Circuit Judge, dissenting:

The undisputed and dispositive fact is that Pedrin was not known to the government to be predisposed to raid a stash house at the time when an agent of the ATF proposed this action to him. The law is settled: "Government agents may not originate a criminal design, implant in an innocent person's mind the disposition to commit a criminal act, and induce commission of a crime so that the government may prosecute." *Jacobson v. United States,* 503 U.S. 540, 548 (1992). In this case, the ATF originated the criminal design, implanted it in Pedrin's mind and induced him to commit the crime that the government then prosecuted.

Who has the burden of proof as to the defendant's disposition? In *Jacobson,* the Supreme Court provided the answer: "[T]he prosecution must prove beyond reasonable doubt that the defendant was disposed to commit the criminal act prior to first being approached by government agents." *Id.* at 549. The timing of the defendant's disposition is critical: "The sole issue is whether the Government met its burden of proving that petitioner was *pre* disposed to violate the law *before* the Government intervened." *Id.* at 549 n. 2 (italics in original).

No showing has been made that Pedrin was known to be predisposed to commit this crime prior to being approached by the agents of ATF. The ATF laid out the entire stash house scheme to him before he had said a single word. The prosecution of his case should be dismissed.

The majority addresses Pedrin's claim of outrageous government conduct—a defense that the Supreme Court has never found to be applicable. The majority does not address entrapment for what would appear to be a good reason: entrapment was not argued by Pedrin. It is within our power to hold that the argument was waived. It is also within our power to notice a meritorious argument unmentioned by counsel. *See Hormel v. Helvering,* 312 U.S. 552, 557 (1941) ("There may always be exceptional cases or particular circumstances which will prompt a reviewing or appellate court, where injustice might otherwise result, to consider questions of law which were neither pressed nor passed upon by the court or administrative agency below."). As a court, we are more than referees tallying scores. We have a live concern that human beings caught in the legal process be treated fairly.

Entrapment is not a defense created by the Constitution or by statute. It is judge-created. It was first recognized by a federal court in a decision of the Ninth Circuit. *Woo Wai v. United States,* 223 F. 412 (9th Cir.1915). It was first recognized by the Supreme Court in *Sorrells v. United States,* 287 U.S. 435 (1932). Entrapment as a defense is the creation of a collaboration between a court and Congress. What Chief Justice Hughes said in *Sorrells* was that Congress could not have intended to punish a man trapped into buying bootleg liquor. Chief Justice Hughes did not cite the legislative history of the National Prohibition Act. What he did was to attribute sensible motivation to the authors of the prohibition law. In his reading they did not intend to criminalize the purchase of the liquor when the purchase was induced by a prohibition agent....

Congress could not have meant the prohibition law should be enforced "by the instigation by government officials of an act on the part of persons otherwise innocent in order to lure them by its commission and to punish them." *Sorrells,* 287 U.S. at 448. Prosecution in such a case was "outside the purview" of the statute and was "abhorrent to the sense of justice." *Id.* at 449. The judgment of conviction was reversed....

*Sorrells* is a live and controlling precedent. The case has been cited 28 times by the Supreme Court, 102 times by this circuit, and 23 times by district courts within the circuit. *Sorrells* has never been overruled or treated as irrelevant. Its central holding has not been challenged. *Sorrells* is an apt precedent for holding the ATF's stash house trick to be entrapment. In fact, the ATF has exceeded the prohibition agent in *Sorrells.* He sold actual liquor. The ATF sponsored the theft of imaginary drugs.

The majority correctly concedes that "[w]hat the government learns only after the fact cannot supply the individualized suspicion that is necessary to justify the sting." Maj. Op. at 797. What did the ATF know about Pedrin before it approached him? The majority does not say. The record says that the ATF knew nothing. It was a shot in the dark when the ATF enlisted Pedrin as a co-conspirator. The majority speaks of a different defendant, Omar Perez, when at page 8 it addresses the question. What the ATF knew of Perez establishes nothing as to what the ATF knew about Pedrin.

Once enlisted, Pedrin recruited others, sketched a scenario for the robbery, and obtained walkie-talkies and scanners. As the ATF had already selected Pedrin as a player in its imagined robbery, none of this activity had any significance. The ATF was already at work with Pedrin cast by the agency as a co-conspirator.

As the case now stands, the ATF enhances its reputation by its successful ruse. The government of the United States is diminished by its dependence on the duplicity of the agency. Because of a choice made by Pedrin or his counsel, entrapment was not argued and *Jacobson* was uncited. By the rules governing litigation we can affirm Pedrin's conviction. By our commitment to a humane justice, we are called to dismiss the case made by the entrappers.

EXCERPTS FROM
*United States v. Pedrin*,
806 F.3d 1009
(9th Cir. 2015)

ORDER

...The petition for rehearing en banc, filed October 15, 2015, is **DENIED.**

NOONAN, Circuit Judge, writing separately to recommend granting the petition for rehearing en banc:

Pedrin argues in his petition for rehearing en banc that the government entrapped him; as set forth in my dissent, *United States v. Pedrin,* 797 F.3d 792, 797–800 (9th Cir.2015), I agree. Additional factors further support Pedrin's claim and I bring them to the forefront here.

The government is guilty of entrapment when it lures a person into committing a crime that he was not predisposed to commit. *Sorrells v. United States,* 287 U.S. 435, 445 (1932). The United States Supreme Court has recognized that when officers of the law engage in this conduct it is "unconscionable, contrary to public policy, and to the established law of the land...." *Id.* at 444–45.

Pedrin asserts that the government lured him into a plan to rob a fictitious stash house by dangling before him a scheme that was "rich in pay off," and involved little work or risk. He further asserts that the government could not establish beyond a reasonable doubt that he was predisposed to participate in the scheme because at the time the government approached him, it had no evidence supporting such a predisposition. *Jacobson v. United States*, 503 U.S. 540, 549 (1992) (holding that the government must prove predisposition beyond a reasonable doubt prior to the government's having approached defendant).

When the government puts psychological pressure on persons to commit a crime this pressure militates towards a finding of entrapment. In *Sorrells*, for example, the Court focused on the fact that the government agent was, like Sorrells, a war veteran who relied on this status in order to pressure Sorrells into getting him liquor. In *Sherman v. United States*, the Court emphasized the psychological pressure the government put on Sherman by relying on an informant who was, like Sherman, a recovering drug addict and who "resort[ed] to sympathy" to persuade Sherman to buy drugs. 356 U.S. 369, 373 (1958). In *Jacobson*, the Court focused on the psychological pressure the government put on Jacobson by repeatedly sending him mailings tempting him to purchase the illegal materials. 503 U.S. at 550.

Here, the government similarly relied on psychological tricks to persuade Pedrin to participate in the crime. First, the confidential informant was co-defendant Omar Perez's uncle, and therefore someone to whom Perez and Pedrin, a close friend of Perez's, were more likely to succumb than they otherwise might. Second, the informant-uncle peer pressured Pedrin and Perez by telling them that the government agent was "very cool people," that he, the informant, "want[ed] to do the job," and that if they could not do it, he would find people who could. Third, the government put time pressure on defendants by telling them the opportunity was available to them for only a limited period. Finally, the government agent eliminated some of the moral qualms defendants may have had about the drug dealers they were planning to rob by telling them that he had "no love" for the dealers and that they were cheating him out of his fair share of the profits from their business. These psychological tactics no less induced defendants to participate in the reverse sting than did the tactics employed by the government in *Sorrells, Sherman*, or *Jacobson*.

Regarding Pedrin's predisposition to participate in the scheme, not only did the government know nothing about him when they approached him, nothing in his record suggests that he was apt to commit a crime like this one. Pedrin was in and out of the juvenile system, and as an adult served time in jail for several misdemeanors. Pedrin had two felony convictions, one for being "belligerent to officers while being booked into jail," and another for the crime of endangerment for which he served a prison sentence of a little over one year.

Pedrin's record contains no crimes related to dealing cocaine, robberies, or home invasions. The only evidence supporting that Pedrin previously committed a stash house robbery is the testimony of co-defendant Terry Bombard who was more than ten years older than twenty-four-year-old Pedrin and who testified against him in exchange for a deal of ten years instead of a life sentence. The government offered no evidence independently corroborating Bombard's testimony. On these facts, Bombard's assertions that Pedrin previously committed stash house robberies would likely not be proven beyond a reasonable doubt.

Because the government employed psychological pressure in luring Pedrin into planning to commit the crime, and because the government could not prove his disposition to commit such a crime beyond a reasonable doubt, I recommend granting the petition for rehearing en banc to consider whether Pedrin was entrapped.

APPENDIX A

# *What It Is Like to Be a Judge* Outline

1. The Electrician Who'd Read the Constitution
2. The Hillsboro Physician
3. The Mocabooboo
4. Find Barrera-Echeverria
5. G'tmo!
6. Horses of the Night
7. The Subversive Washerwoman

| | THEMES |
|---|---|
| 1. Intent | (a) Folk psychology<br>(b) Neuroscience |
| 2. Jurisdiction | A limit on power and a limit on responsibility |
| 3. Values and Logic | (a) balance<br>(b) oxymoron |
| 4. Assuming the truth | (a) Dismissal<br>(b) Summary Judgement<br>(c) Appeals |
| 5. The King's Judges? | |
| 6. The Psychology of the Courtroom | (a) Architecture<br>(b) Layout<br>(c) Dress |

| | |
|---|---|
| 7. The Exercise of Power | (a) Sentencing<br>(b) Appeals |
| 8. The Diplomacy of Judges | |
| 9. Judges and Lawyers | |
| 10. Judges and Law Clerks | |
| 11. Judges As Models | (a) Cardozo; Hand, Jackson<br>(b) Colleagues |
| 12. Judges and Litigants | |
| 13. Judges and Critics | |
| 14. Judges and Congress | |
| 15. Judges and The Executive | |
| 16. Judges and The INS | |
| 17. Does The Judge Make A Difference? | |
| 18. Judges As Friends | |
| 19. A Sense of Proportion | |
| 20. Original Meaning And The Letter Of The Law | |
| 21. Text And Context | |
| 22. Judge Not, Lest You Be Judged | |
| 23. The Secret Of The System | |
| 24. Impersonality | |
| 25. Complicity | |
| 26. Satisfaction | |
| 27. Legal Language | (a) Euphemisms<br>(b) Latinisms |

APPENDIX B

# April 2, 2013 Foreword

The Supreme Court of the United States appropriately receives the most public scrutiny and the most professional analyses. The twelve intermediate federal courts are not so well known and not so closely examined.[1] Appointments to them receive comparatively little attention. The particular characteristics of each of these courts are often not remarked. With a few exceptions the judges have the anonymity of appointees to any agency of the federal government. The facts of the cases decided are regularly not reported in the press.

In this book, I seek to show how the Ninth Circuit, the busiest of the twelve, does its work or at least how I, a judge of this court for twenty-seven years, have done my share of its work. Aren't the opinions and dissents I've written the best evidence? Why add to them? I answer that these formal filings need informed commentary to communicate the judge's sense of the interplay of persons and rules

No one can give an insightful account of a case without referring to the rules governing it. No one can give such an account without attention to the actors in it. The lawyers, the litigants, the judges, all partake in the process in which persons apply rules to other persons.

The process is not the march of rules determining a conclusion the way mathematical rules lead to answer. The process is not the milling about of human beings without boundaries or directions. The persons

1. Judge Noonan clearly had in mind the twelve federal appeals courts that have a territorial jurisdiction. The jurisdiction of the Court of Appeals for the Federal Circuit is based on subject matter and it can hear appeals from any federal district court as well as various federal agencies.

we restrict by rules to particular roles. Yet a courtroom is not a theater. At least some of the participants in the process will be affected by it—enriched or impoverished, acquitted or condemned to imprisonment or to death, admitted to the country or expelled from it. That human beings triumph or suffer as an accessory consequence of their part in the process means that we who shape it must try to understand it and make it better.

APPENDIX C

# September 8, 2013 Foreword

In 2012, to my real surprise, my court, the Ninth Circuit, became the target of political assault, scorn, and proposed abolition. For over seventy years the Ninth Circuit had been the object of political grumbling, chiefly by senators from the northwestern states within the circuit who detected a California bias in its rulings. When Alaska became a state and acquired senators the grumbling had increased. A favorite solution was to split the circuit. No one had cried, "Écrasez l'infame." But now "rogue court" was what my court was being called. Its extinction was being advocated as part of a political agenda.

These attacks were made far from the Ninth Circuit by political figures living far from the circuit.[1] The attacks functioned to advance political causes without perceptible effect on our work. Yet it is useful to dispel the mythology on which such political discourse depends. So I have decided to call this book Ninth Circuit! and to show the ways through which our court works.

The Ninth Circuit is the federal court of appeals for lawsuits brought in nine western states—Alaska, Arizona, California, Hawaii, Idaho, Montana, Nevada, Oregon and Washington. This area is inhabited by over 60 million persons. Our court hears appeals from judgments in civil suits and criminal cases decided by the federal district courts. Our court also hears appeals from the Board of Immigration Appeals and other federal admin-

---

1. As part of their criticisms of the court, in 2012 two prominent public figures seeking nomination as a major-party presidential candidate called for the Ninth Circuit to be broken up or abolished. *See, e.g.,*, John P. Freeman, *Protecting Judicial Independence*, 6 Charleston L. Rev. 511, 515 (2012).

istrative agencies such as the National Labor Relations Board which have ruled on issues arising within the nine states. A third source of appeals for us are decisions of state criminal courts challenged by prisoners claiming that the federal Constitution has been violated by the state courts. These claims relate to criminal convictions but are styled as civil actions because the federal court imposes no criminal penalty.

Congress has determined our court's size—29 active judges when the court is at full strength. The active judges are supplemented by judges who have taken "senior status," meaning that they have reached a point where their age plus years of service equal 80. At that point they may retire at full salary, or continue to serve as active judges, or choose a less demanding schedule in senior status. The present court has 27 active judges and 16 judges in senior status, making it the largest federal court in the country.

Of the active judges, the chief judge and one other were appointed by President Reagan. Two were appointed by President Carter. Eleven were appointed by President Clinton. Seven were appointed by President George W. Bush. Five were appointed by President Obama. Chance, not politics, has largely determined when a vacancy occurred and therefore who made the appointment.

Who made the appointment is always relevant but not necessarily a decisive fact. A court is not a political arena. Neither is it insulated from all political currents. It is likely that a judicial appointee will share the political outlook of the president making the appointment. That does not assure identity of outlook among those appointees. Sometimes judges prove to be independent of political allegiance or outlook. Occasionally, as a way of getting one appointment approved by Congress, a president will agree to appoint a judge favored by the other party.

As I see the present roster, I would identify ten of the active judges as conservative, fourteen as liberal, and three as not easily catalogued. Of the judges in senior status, I would say that seven are conservative, seven are liberal, and two evade classification. Any combination of three—active or senior—may by lot be chosen to constitute a panel. The possibility, therefore, exists of a completely conservative panel or a completely liberal panel. A mixed panel is more likely.[2]

---

2. The following two paragraphs on the Ninth Circuit's en banc practice have been inserted from a separate, short document, because they seem to fit naturally here. Unlike

En bancs control and correct the aberrant decisions of panels. A case goes en banc only if a majority of the active judges voted take it en banc. Senior status judges are only eligible to be drawn to sit on an en banc if they were originally on the panel deciding the case. They are also not eligible to vote on whether to take a case en banc. These restrictions result in active judges dominating the en banc process.

As can be seen from my estimate, neither conservatives nor liberals have enough votes to get a case en banc. Once that happens neither group has any assurance as to which ones of them will be drawn from a wooden box containing small balls, each bearing the name of an active or senior judge. An en banc court could be drawn of eleven conservatives or of eleven liberals. It is not likely. Given a slight plurality of conservatives, the likelihood is that an en banc court will be more conservative than the three-judge panel which first decided the case. En bancs are relatively rare—about 20 a year in a court whose panels decide about 6,000 cases.[3]

The cases that come before us have various sources. No single theme or thread ties them together. This book reflects the vigorous variety that results. I do offer a unity of perspective. I have chosen these thirteen[4] cases because, taken together, they illustrate the character of the appeals we hear, the problems and puzzlements of the process of judging them, and the certainties and uncertainties attendant on this process. Each of them is viewed from the same perspective—my perspective as a judge who participated in the decision.

A judge's job is to affix responsibility—responsibility for a crime, a tort, a default, an error. The judge regularly places responsibility on the persons before the court. In this book, I seek to affix responsibility on the judge. Is the judge then to be judged? Why not? Self-judgment is not barred by judicial immunity.

---

the other United States courts of appeals, when the 9th Circuit sits "en banc," it does so through a randomly chosen panel of eleven judges rather than through the full court. In theory, the full court could decide to rehear, with all eligible judges sitting, a case decided by an en banc panel, although it does not appear that the Ninth Circuit has ever done so. *See Abebe v. Holder*, 577 F.3d 1113, 1113–14 (9th Cir. 2009) (Berzon, Cir. J., dissenting from denial of full court rehearing)

3. The inserted document ends here.

4. The manuscript reads "fifteen."

No judge acts alone. The judge is in a system whose rules must be followed, cooperating with colleagues chosen by others, interacting with lawyers who are essential to the judge's work but who are not appointed by the judge. It is with keen appreciation of the context provided by this system that I maintain that the person who is a judge makes a difference. A judge may be cold or kind, modest or self-assertive, gregarious or a loner. No need to enumerate the possibilities open to any human being. Once a person is a judge in the case, the identity of that person becomes a focus.

Why would anyone see the judge as focal? The judge may not possess the power of a corporate litigant or the resources of a great government bureaucracy. The judge may lack the rhetorical ability of an advocate or the cunning of sophisticated counsel. Nonetheless, to the attentive observer of the legal process, the judge makes a difference.

If, in actuality, litigation were decided by a computer, one could disregard the decision-making human. Computer programs, however, are not today an acceptable tool for determining a just result.

"The judge is a lazy fellow." Austin Scott, Dane Professor of Law at Harvard Law School and my teacher, used to say.[5] I heard him make the remark enough times for it to be stored in my memory and to make me ask, "Is it true?" Scott's remark was not applied by him to any particular laggard. His judgment was generic. The lawyers were the busy people in a court. They put the case together, assembled the pertinent documents, interviewed and examined the witnesses, raised objections, and argued the issues. The judge made rulings as the lawyers prompted him. Compared to the multi-tasked lawyers, the judge reigned like a deity, uninvolved in the disappointments and frustrations, the anxieties and hopes of those over whom the judge presided.

Scott's saying I now read as the tactic of a teacher trying to convey to his students a sense of what their responsibilities would be as lawyers. It was not a judgment on judges. I know from experience that a judge is a busy person.

The judge is a person interacting with other persons—his colleagues, the lawyers in the case, and the litigants, whom an appeals court may not even see. The interaction involves rules that define the roles of the partic-

---

5. See Appendix E for a somewhat different version of Judge Noonan's reflections on Professor Scott's saying.

ipants in the process and rules determining the law governing the case. A judge is given authority by his role. A judge is given direction by the law. Neither role nor law exhausts nor extinguishes the judge as person. A human being, the judge is not merely a role-player applying legal rules.

An analogy with baseball suggests itself.[6] Each player is assigned to a position. A first baseman is not to catch balls on the third base side. Each position is limited and exclusive. Yet individual players are larger than their positions. A Lou Gehrig is more than a first baseman; a Buster Posey is more than a catcher. The game has to be understood not only in terms of the positions but in terms of the persons playing them.

Baseball offers a familiar and homely analogy to a lawsuit. The analogy limps, however, because it leaves out of account the impact that rules in a legal system have upon human beings. By rule in baseball, a batter will be out for the inning if his fly is caught. By rule in a legal system, a burglar will be in for six years if he is convicted. Systems with such substantially different outcomes should be examined separately.

No game is a fit analogy when we recognize that the acts of judges decide who shall be the parents of a child, who shall inherit the estate of an ancestor, who shall go to prison, who shall be expelled from the country, who shall be put to death. The acts of judges touch persons. Acting upon other persons, judges are responsible as persons for these acts.[7]

---

6. In a separate, short document labeled "The Game Analogy," Noonan explored different sports analogies, specifically to a trial:

> Most Americans like sports, at least enough to watch them. It is easy to think of a trial as a kind of sport. It is a contest. There are two or more contestants. There is a referee. There is a winner and a loser. What sport is more like a trial?
>
> Not golf, the interactions are not quick enough. Not tennis, the referee's role is too limited. Soccer and basketball are real candidates. In each the ball is moving most of the time and the referee has some discretion.

7. The following two paragraphs have been inserted from a separate document labelled "Insert A" because they provide a meaningful conclusion to the September 2013 foreword. However, Insert A's use of a baseball analogy may make that a questionable decision; Judge Noonan clearly was both drawn to and uneasy about any game analogy. The reader must judge.

In two of these thirteen cases,[8] professional counsel had not mattered—the case of the electrician defending himself and the case of the three-strikes prisoner arguing his own appeal. In the other cases, as typically happens, counsel were important to the result we reached. Two cases were federal criminal cases, in one of which I upheld a light sentence (the aberrant act case) and in one I thought the Fourth Amendment had been violated and my view was vindicated by the Supreme Court (the case of the heat machine). In one habeas case, that of Harris, I believed that habeas should be granted but did not persuade the Supreme Court. In another state habeas case, Ramirez's, I joined in giving relief to the state prisoner. In one federal case, that of Barrera, I thought an alien held indefinitely in prison should be released, and my view of the law was upheld by the Supreme Court in a later case. In one criminal case, that of the sacramental confession, I wrote an opinion safeguarding the sacrament without the slightest impact on the state criminal case. In a federal extradition case, Into the Maze, I intruded into another panel's case without success. In three civil cases with no criminal implications, those of Her Voice, Herself, The Hillsboro Physician, and the Mocababoo, I wrote opinions that sustained, or authorized, damages for the plaintiffs.

If I may tum to baseball to create a score, my batting average in this small sample was .716. There were three unsuccessful dissents. A legal mind will note that I picked these cases to write about. Is my average, over-all, that good? I haven't tried to calculate it. I do know that, as in baseball, no judge has a perfect average, that to err is human, and that judges do err. I have set down what seem to me characteristics of the Ninth Circuit.

8. The manuscript reads "fourteen."

APPENDIX D

# Foreword Fragments

I have no doubt law can be used to inflict injustice. How could anyone think otherwise? Law was used to create slavery in Rome and the Roman Empire, in China and the Chinese Empire, and in the United States prior to 1865. Laws had authorized the use of torture in most of the countries of medieval Europe and at least between 1540 and 1640 in England. Law has left governments free to characterize certain activities as acts of state beyond judicial inspection or control.

Earlier, in a book I called *Persons and Masks of the Law*, I distinguished between persons, roles, and masks. Persons were flesh and blood and soul, touchable human beings. Roles were the particular parts the persons played in society, parts defined by law or custom. Mask was a metaphor I chose to express suppression by law of the human identity of the person playing the role. At one end of the social scale, the mask of property had for centuries suppressed the human identity of a slave. As property, he or she could be owned, bought, sold, and used as a tool without the user acknowledging the human person affected. The legal mask, almost perfectly, obscured that person.

At the other end of society, the mask of sovereignty hid those exercising the powers of government. A sovereign was not accountable for certain of his acts. As the embodiment, the sovereign was immune. Again, focus on the mask created by law almost perfectly concealed the human actor behind it.

There were also, I had suggested, less complete masks provided by legal systems—Plaintiffs and defendants, for example. Analyzing cases in terms of Ps and Ds permitted a law teacher to ignore the individuality of litigants while expounding a rule. Similarly, a judge's thought could move from the persons to classes of Ps and Ds. The line between a mask and a role was imprecise. Roles could be turned, more or less effectively, into masks. But roles were as essential as rules to the functioning of a society. Masks were a problem and a plague. I argued that a fuller and better understanding of a case was achieved by taking into account the actual participants, the persons who were submerged in categories. Being a law professor and not a judge at the time I did not note the mask of the judge. Taught by experience, I am now conscious of the judge's...

* * *

Before becoming a judge, I had known Frank Good, a superior court judge, my father's close friend, always available and kind. I had some sense of Hugh McLellan, a monument of integrity. I had met George Sweeney, the father of Sheila, and John Spalding, the father of Marianne. Knowing the daughters did not translate into understanding the work of the fathers. I did know something about judicial business from teaching law. I had little sense of the day-to-day routine. I believe that when I was appointed to the Ninth Circuit, I visualized myself on the bench five days a week.

* * *

Ultimately, no doubt, our society as a whole is responsible for the litigation that occurs within it. More specifically, the laws of the country are responsible. Narrower still, responsibility rests with the judicial system. These responsibilities are beyond the range of my book. I look at the judges who acted in the cases I set out. In the first-person memoir, the first person responsible can only be myself.

In each of these cases, once I had arrived at a conclusion, I cared a great deal that the conclusion should prevail. Why? As the saying goes, it was no skin off my nose whoever won or lost. The addition of a few million dollars to Sun or the release of Barrera-Echavarria from prison did not affect my assets or my health. As far as any tangible consequence was concerned, I might as well having been dealing with denizens of another planet.

Once after deliberation I'd reached a conclusion, I was committed to it as fair and final. It was my conclusion as a judge and as a person. Adhesion to my own assessment of the case, after I'd been outvoted or overruled, was something more than a stubborn unwillingness to admit I'd made a mistake. It was a conviction that the system had malfunctioned. A judge, I was bound by the system. A person, I had not lost my capacity to reach a personal conclusion. In this book, I offer four cases where I disagreed with the result the system reached.

The narrative begins with my first years as a judge and ends with this year, my twenty-seventh. Only one judicial experience has been such that I never wanted to repeat it. It is described in chapter 12, "Losing Robert Alton Harris," in which I speak of my role in a case where death was imposed on the petitioner before us.

In an article in The New Yorker entitled "Tinkering With Death," and subtitled "Personal History" and "A death-penalty judge reflects: How does it feel to send another man to die?," my colleague Alex Kozinski expressed the doubts and hesitations he has had as a judge asked to stop the infliction of death upon a convicted murderer. As he recalls, "it began to sink in that Baal really was going to die and that I would have played a part in ending his life." Nonetheless, he participated in the case and continues to participate in such cases: "I do it because I believe that society is entitled to take the life of those who have shown utter contempt for the lives of others. And because I hear the tortured voices of the victims crying out for vindication."[1]

In the case of Harris, as the reader will see, I thought his sanity at the time of his crime was in doubt and I thought that the method of execution was open to challenge as cruel and unusual. I did not vote to spare Harris out of principled opposition to the death penalty but out of fidelity to due process of law. Because death was about to be imposed by the state, the pressure was palpable.

Why is impatience with delay so often characteristic of death penalty cases? It is not that the condemned criminal is likely to escape. It is not

---

1. *See* Kozinski, *Tinkering With Death: A Death-Penalty Judge Reflects: How Does It Feel To Send Another Man To Die?*, New Yorker, Feb. 10, 1997.

that the legal process is notably more complex and tedious than in many hard-fought civil cases.

Speculating, I would say that there is something about the deliberate killing of a human being that makes those connected with it anxious to be done with it. The prosecutors, of course, want their work to be over. But what moves the judges?

In the case of Harris, I did not think of myself as "a deathpenalty judge." No judge of our court had imposed any penalty. We were being asked to intervene, but our very limited role kept us from being accessories to his death. The law is full of distinctions based on one's responsibility for an act.

...a prosecutor may seek the penalty of death and a judge may impose it.

"[All] judges are in some way people of violence," Robert Cover has written. I read his statement as rhetorical exaggeration. To apply force is not to apply violence.[2]

---

2. Robert M. Cover, *Nomos and Narrative*, 97 Harv. L. Rev. 4, 47 (1983). Judge Noonan described Professor Cover elsewhere as a "brilliant teacher and writer, humane defender of human obligations to God." John T. Noonan, Jr., *Horses of the Night: Harris v. Vasquez*, 45 Stan. L. Rev. 1011, 1011 n. a (1993). *See also id.* at 1022–23:

> "[A]ll judges are in some way people of violence," Robert Cover has written. They apply violence on behalf of the state. I do not wholly agree with this rhetoric. Judges only occasionally have to apply force, and when lawful force is employed, it is distinguishable from the unregulated brutality that the term "violence" suggests. But a judge who does order that a man be put to death is a cooperator in the use of lethal force. So, too, are those who approve the order on appeal. There is nothing sinful or shameful in such collaboration if the death penalty is morally justified.
>
> What about the federal judges, who neither impose the sentence nor affirm it? Their role restricts them. They can only say whether the federal constitution has been violated by the trial and sentencing. Role responsibility is real responsibility. The judges are not free to dispense their own view of justice. They cannot act as prophets.

Judge Noonan returned to the issues of power, force and violence in judging in a later essay.

> What is meant by power in the legal context? It is not the physical force of a steam engine. It is not water power or electrical power. Yet it seems to have an impact and leave an imprint. No metric measures it, but at times the impact is palpable, cutting through the paper

morass, touching the flesh, the fortune, the home, the existence of the persons it reaches.

Courts do issue mandates. But most of a judicial decision is not a command, but an act of reasoning and persuading. A justice is not a general. The judges in the legal system are not soldiers.

"You have the power." The speaker was Byron White, an associate justice of the United States Supreme Court. The addressees were a group of judges recently appointed to the federal circuit courts. The implication of Justice White's remark was that the real power lay not with the Supreme Court, able to handle a minuscule number of cases a year. The power is with the circuits that decided fifty thousand or more. Like almost all participants in the power conferred by law, Justice White was convinced that its exercise was mostly enjoyed by someone other than himself....

Within the panel of three that will address the issues on appeal to my court there is a further diminution of power. Each judge has one vote. The presiding judge has the power of assigning the opinion but may lose this power if the panel divides and he or she is the dissenter. The one who writes the opinion must retain the vote of at least one member. The opinion is not the expression of a single mind.

The power of a circuit court judge, then, cannot be visualized as the power of a man with a gun that can shoot at will, or the power of a dictator able to declare what is the law. Power as material energy is applied by multiple human interactions. The application is made through means that depend for their operation on human language, memory, and reasoning. The power exercised by the judge will have physical consequences: the transfer of money, the release or jailing or deportation of another person, even an execution. But the exercise of power itself is by a communication. It is in the realm of words that analogies to it must be found or distinguished....

The place of power should not be exaggerated. Law can coerce. But often it offers options. You can combine your assets with another and make a contract. You can pool your assets with others and form a corporation to do business or bestow charity. You can bequeath your assets to anyone. No law will compel you to adopt any of these options. The law creates the opportunity. The law channels your choice, providing forms for action.

The law also is constantly teaching—teaching not only in the imprecise and habitual ways that law enlists the law-abiding person, but teaching precisely by procedural rules meant for professionals. What are most judicial opinions but pedagogy for lawyers and judges? A few lines conveys whatever power is at work. Most of an opinion is reasoning directed at minds.

John T. Noonan, Jr., *Through Papers to Persons*, 55 Vill. L. Rev. 1121, 1125–27 (2010).

APPENDIX E

# "The Judge Is A Lazy Fellow"

The title of this chapter[1] was a saying of Austin Scott, Dane Professor of Law at Harvard Law School, preeminent oracle on the law of trusts, and my teacher. I heard him make the remark enough times for it to be stored in my memory and make me ask now, "Is it true?" Professor Scott did not speak of any particular laggard. His comment was generic. By role the judge was lazy.

The busy people were the lawyers. They put the case together, assembled the documents, presented the witnesses, raised the objections, and argued to the court. The judge sat and listened. The judge ruled as the lawyers informed him he should. Compared to the multi-tasked lawyers for the litigants, the judge was a benign deity, uninvolved in the emotions of the litigants, inactive unless stimulated to action by a lawyer.

I suppose that such trial judges may exist and that even panels of appellate judges may harbor those in this category. They are not the judges of my experience. I now understand Professor Scott's remark as a pedagogic ploy, meant to tell law students that they would have a lot to do as lawyers. Professor Scott was too wise an oracle to take his own comment literally.

As I look back at the cases I've set out, I doubt that laziness has been my vice. I was not just a member of a courtroom audience in any of them. At the same time, I've not been free to shape the courtroom drama

1. In the main manuscript, this document follows chapter 10, "The Heat Machine." But as the latest, September 8 version of the foreword shows, Judge Noonan had rethought the idea of interrupting the series of case accounts with an essay of a different kind.

as though I'd written the play. My part has been to play a role, a role circumscribed by responsibilities and rules.

That it has been a role and that the role has been limited by rules are facts not relieving me of personal accountability for my actions. A judge cannot say that someone else ordered him to find a person guilty, to disregard a defense, or to deny the liability of a tortfeasor. What is true of ultimate decisions in a case is equally true of subsidiary decisions such as admitting or excluding evidence. A judge is accountable for each and every one of his rulings that affect the lives, liberty or property of the litigants. The judge is not calling balls and strikes in a game.[2] The judge's acts are those of a human person touching, in a variety of ways, other human persons.

Now no doubt the judge's role requires many of his acts. Where his role restricts his action, he cannot go beyond it, for example, to grant the habeas petition of a prisoner whose conviction has been obtained in a matter not held unconstitutional by the United States Supreme Court. The result may be wrong in the judgment of the judge, but he cannot throw off his role any more than on the bench he can throw off his robe. To the extent that he is a judge his role defines him.

Yet the judge is a person, that is flesh and blood and soul with, in my belief, a destiny beyond this earth. The judge, as person, does not cease to be accountable to God. If the judicial system in which the judge takes

---

2. Judge Noonan presumably had in mind the much-discussed remarks Chief Justice John G. Roberts, Jr., made in testifying before the Senate Judiciary Committee during his confirmation process. Roberts said:

> Judges and Justices are servants of the law, not the other way around. Judges are like umpires. Umpires don't make the rules, they apply them. The role of an umpire and a judge is critical. They make sure everybody plays by the rules, but it is a limited role. Nobody ever went to a ball game to see the umpire....
>
> I have no agenda, but I do have a commitment. If I am confirmed, I will confront every case with an open mind. I will fully and fairly analyze the legal arguments that are presented. I will be open to the considered views of my colleagues on the bench, and I will decide every case based on the record, according to the rule of law, without fear or favor, to the best of my ability, and I will remember that it's my job to call balls and strikes, and not to pitch or bat.

Confirmation Hearing on the Nomination of John G. Roberts, Jr. to be Chief Justice of the United States: Hearing Before the S. Comm. on the Judiciary, 109th Cong. 56 (2005).

his place were as corrupt as the National Socialist regime of Germany, the judge would have no choice but to resign his role.

The extreme case may seem easy, although no doubt in practice it is hard to recognize the extreme case. But what of a system that does not do systematic injustice and yet is at times unjust? When I was teaching Professional Responsibility to Boalt students, I would assure them that every human system is sometimes unjust, and they would have to decide at some point whether they were cooperating in injustice.

I continue to believe what I told the Boalt students. I have occasionally asked myself whether the system in which I play a role is such that I am cooperating in injustice.

American judges are not clothed in wigs and ermine like their British predecessors. Nor are they feted on circuits by the local notables as circuit judges were in England. They are not immune from impeachment by Congress but it has happened only fifteen times in history. They are not immune from punishment for criminal acts, but that has happened only very rarely.[3] They can be persuaded or pressured to resign on account of some failure to function as judges. On the whole, they are secure in their jobs. They are the only federal appointees, except the Librarian of Congress, whose tenure is not terminated by age or years of service. Their appointments are good for life. That is their security and their isolation from financial pressures. Add that, by terms of Article III of the Constitution, their salaries can never be reduced. The provision doesn't protect them from the effects of inflation. It does protect them from any vindictive reaction of Congress.

---

3. In the manuscript, the last two sentences read: "They are not immune from impeachment by Congress but it has happened only six times in history. They are not immune from punishment for criminal acts, but that has happened only [blank]." As of August 2025, fifteen Article III judges have been impeached by the House of Representatives, eight of whom were convicted by the Senate and removed from office. Three others resigned while the impeachment proceedings were ongoing. https://www.fjc.gov/history/judges/impeachments-federal-judges. The number of federal judges convicted of a crime in ordinary criminal proceedings is unclear but very small.

APPENDIX F

# Should State Executions Run on Schedule?

## *N.Y. Times, April 27, 1992, at A17*

"Treason to the Constitution" is a strong charge. It was the phrase employed in 1821 in argument before Chief Justice John Marshall to describe a Federal court's failure to exercise its jurisdiction in a case properly brought before it. On Saturday evening, April 18, a courageous Federal judge, Marilyn Hall Patel, refused to commit treason to the Constitution and, in a suit brought under the Civil Rights Act, ordered a hearing on whether death by cyanide gas was cruel and unusual punishment prohibited by the Constitution. Her order also affected the execution of Robert Alton Harris, the condemned murderer scheduled to die on April 21. The state immediately appealed to my court, the Ninth Circuit.

The established standards, built up over the years by the judiciary, are these: First, "cruel and unusual" means "cruel and unusual" in today's terms. Not even the most doctrinaire "original intent" jurist maintains that the determination is to be made as of 1791, when the Bill of Rights became part of the Constitution. Since Weems v. United States in 1909, we have been committed to an evolving standard of human decency.

Second, a good index of what is cruel and unusual is what the state legislatures allow. In 1992, just three states authorize cyanide gas as the only means of inflicting capital punishment. One, Arizona, is in the process of abandoning the method, and another, Maryland, has not had an execution since 1961. It is a serious question whether the consensus of all the other legislatures shows that California's means of carrying out the death penalty violates the constitutional norm.

Third, any "unnecessary suffering" in imposing the death penalty is forbidden by the Constitution. The Constitution permits capital punishment; it does not permit torture. Judge Patel was presented Saturday night with a mass of affidavits asserting that the use of the gas chamber did lead to a tortured death. It is an important question whether this evidence could be rebutted.

Concluding as a matter of common sense that these questions could not be answered on a Saturday night, Judge Patel set a hearing to be held in 10 days where testimony could be taken and the arguments, pro and con, fully explored. Pending the hearing, she prohibited the use of lethal gas to execute anyone. The immediate beneficiary was Robert Alton Harris.

He was only one of 323 death-row inmates in California on whose behalf the civil rights action was brought. The state, anxious for him to meet his date with death, claimed that the case was really "a Harris case," unfairly brought at the last moment to throw his execution off track. The state's contention brought into focus an issue now before the country—not the death penalty itself, but whether the precedents, built up over this century for guarding everyone's civil rights, are to be suspended or set aside to assure the orderly keeping of an execution date. About 3 A.M. on Tuesday, the U.S. Supreme Court decided that the Harris execution must stay on track. Federal courts must no longer exercise their jurisdiction in ways that would derail it.

Profound ambivalence had existed. We are a country with a Constitution and a Bill of Rights, which we celebrate and cherish and which the courts enforce. We are a country with a Civil Rights Act that no one wants to appeal. But we are also a country where some states by vote have determined that atrocious crimes may be punished by death.

Prompt enforcement of that penalty conflicts with the precedents built up under the Constitution, Bill of Rights and Civil Rights Act. If death penalties are to be inflicted according to a state's schedule, these protections must give way. A Federal court must even commit "treason to the Constitution" and abstain from exercising its jurisdiction.

So, at least, is the present position of the U.S. Supreme Court, Justices Harry A. Blackmun and John Paul Stevens dissenting. That Court has resolved the national ambivalence and decided that it is intolerable for a Federal court to delay an execution to decide a constitutional question. Robert Alton Harris was a casualty of this decision. Was the Constitution, too?

# Index